ACCIDENTS

IN NORTH AMERICAN MOUNTAINEERING 2015

the
**AMERICAN
ALPINE** club

AMERICAN ALPINE CLUB
GOLDEN, COLORADO

ALPINE CLUB OF CANADA
CANMORE, ALBERTA

ISSN: 0065-028X
ISBN: 978-1-933056-89-0
ISBN (e-book): 978-1-933056-90-6

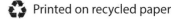 Printed on recycled paper

Manufactured in the United States. Published by the American Alpine Club, 710 Tenth Street, Suite 100, Golden, CO, 80401, *www.americanalpineclub.org*.

PHOTOS

[Front Cover] A climber reaches for an old piton. *Photo by Andrew Burr.*

[Page 1] Climbing in the North Cascades, Washington. *Photo by Obadiah Reid.*

[Table of Contents] Titcomb Basin, Wyoming. *Photo by Mark Evans.*

[Back Cover] Rescue from Camp V on the Nose of El Capitan. *Photo by Tom Evans / Elcapreport.com*

WARNING!

The activities described within *Accidents in North American Mountaineering (ANAM)*—including but not limited to: rock climbing, ice climbing, mountaineering, backcountry skiing, or any other outdoor activity—carry a significant risk of personal injury or death. The owners, staff, contributors, and volunteers that create this publication recommend that you DO NOT participate in these activities unless you are an expert, have sought or obtained qualified professional instruction or guidance, are knowledgeable about the risks involved, and are willing to assume personal responsibility for all the risks associated with these activities. ANAM and its publisher, the American Alpine Club, MAKE NO WARRANTIES, EXPRESSED OR IMPLIED, OF ANY KIND REGARDING THE CONTENTS OF THIS PUBLICATION, AND EXPRESSLY DISCLAIM ANY WARRANTY REGARDING THE ACCURACY OR RELIABILITY OF INFORMATION CONTAINED HEREIN. The American Alpine Club further disclaims any responsibility for injuries or death incurred by any person engaging in these activities. Use the information contained in this publication at your own risk, and do not depend on the information contained herein for personal safety or for determining whether to attempt any climb, route, or activity described herein. The examples/stories contained herein are anecdotal and/ or informational only and not intended to represent advice, recommendations, or commentary on appropriate conduct, standards or choices that you, the reader, may make regarding your own activities.

METEOR

Artfully engineered
to take (and make) an impact.

**Lightweight, breathable climbing and
mountaineering helmet**

Light on the head and very airy thanks to generous
ventilation, the new METEOR helmet offers exceptional
comfort and protection for rock, ice, and alpine use.
The simple adjustment system and magnetic chinstrap
buckle offer unparalleled ease of use.
Available in two sizes, to fit a wide array of users.

Access
the
inaccessible

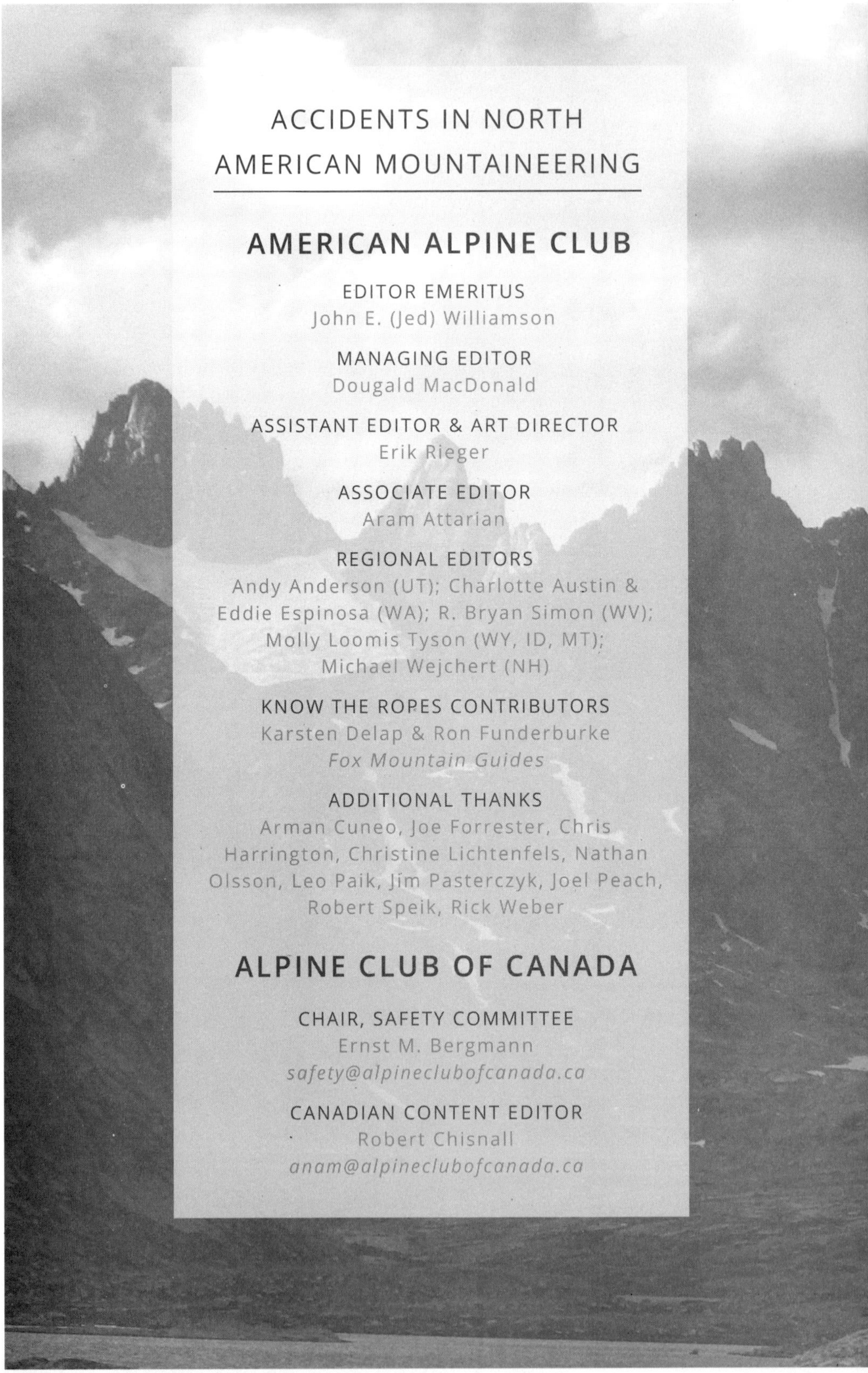

ACCIDENTS IN NORTH AMERICAN MOUNTAINEERING

AMERICAN ALPINE CLUB

EDITOR EMERITUS
John E. (Jed) Williamson

MANAGING EDITOR
Dougald MacDonald

ASSISTANT EDITOR & ART DIRECTOR
Erik Rieger

ASSOCIATE EDITOR
Aram Attarian

REGIONAL EDITORS
Andy Anderson (UT); Charlotte Austin &
Eddie Espinosa (WA); R. Bryan Simon (WV);
Molly Loomis Tyson (WY, ID, MT);
Michael Wejchert (NH)

KNOW THE ROPES CONTRIBUTORS
Karsten Delap & Ron Funderburke
Fox Mountain Guides

ADDITIONAL THANKS
Arman Cuneo, Joe Forrester, Chris
Harrington, Christine Lichtenfels, Nathan
Olsson, Leo Paik, Jim Pasterczyk, Joel Peach,
Robert Speik, Rick Weber

ALPINE CLUB OF CANADA

CHAIR, SAFETY COMMITTEE
Ernst M. Bergmann
safety@alpineclubofcanada.ca

CANADIAN CONTENT EDITOR
Robert Chisnall
anam@alpineclubofcanada.ca

2015 · VOLUME 10 · NUMBER 5 · ISSUE 68

CONTENTS

PREFACE

THE 68TH ANNUAL EDITION

BY DOUGALD MACDONALD, *MANAGING EDITOR*

Longtime readers will notice subtle but important changes to this year's edition of *Accidents*, especially an increase in photos and diagrams. Our goal is not simply to dress up these pages but more to provide instructional information and visual context for accidents. In many cases, a picture truly is worth a thousand words.

Less visible but equally important is an expanding team of volunteer regional editors. We've enlisted local experts from Washington to West Virginia to seek out and edit the most informative accident reports in their areas, and also serve as *Accidents* ambassadors to nearby parks and SAR teams. This team will grow to cover the entire United States, adding local knowledge and personal relationships to our coverage, in much the same way as longtime volunteer Aram Attarian has done this in the Southeast. If you have a passion for climbing safety and an interest in journalistic coverage of accidents, you may be able to help in your area. Ask me for details at *accidents@americanalpineclub.org*.

Accidents will continue to evolve in three other ways that will become more prominent in the coming year. First and foremost, we will be publishing reports much earlier at our website: *publications.americanalpineclub.org*. Instead of waiting a full year for a new edition of *Accidents*, you will find reports online as soon as they are fully researched and edited. (Did you know that you can already search more than 4,000 accident reports at the website?) We also plan expanded online stories, using additional media to explain complicated incidents. And we'll be working to make our statistics more useful and accessible to climbers and researchers.

All of these initiatives build on the remarkable legacy of Jed Williamson, who retired last year after 40 years at the helm of *Accidents*. If you have suggestions or comments, write to me at *accidents@americanalpineclub.org*.

CONTRIBUTE

SUBMISSIONS

Accidents in North American Mountaineering depends upon detailed incident reports from injured climbers, their partners, search and rescue organizations, and park officials. First-person reports or analyses of climbing accidents or near misses are always welcome. Visit *publications.americanalpineclub.org/accidents_submission* to file a report online or email *accidents@americanalpineclub.org* to learn more.

GIFTS

Accidents also depends on financial contributions from climbers. Your donations support this book and the rapid expansion of our online resources. Gifts of $250 or more will be acknowledged in next year's edition. Email Keegan Young at *kyoung@americanalpineclub.org* to get involved.

THE DYNAMIC

Beal Athlete, Jewell Lund on the initial ice couloir of the Colton-Leach, Mount Huntington, Alaska. Photo: Chantel Astorga

CLIMBING EDUCATION

A NEW CHAPTER AT THE AAC

BY PHIL POWERS, *AMERICAN ALPINE CLUB CEO*

Have you ever agreed to climb with new partners but wondered whether their safety skills were adequate? Have you taken a climbing class but wondered about the instructor's qualifications?

At the American Alpine Club, we believe that climbers in the United States would benefit from consistent, standardized instruction.

This new direction for the AAC began in 2013 when we started hearing from our members—lots of them—that safety education was the number one missing piece in our slate of programs. Around that same time we adopted a vision statement that calls for a "united community of competent climbers." Since then we have been laying the foundation to institute a new arm of the organization that will focus on climber education and safety. Today, we are finalizing curricula for the most common essential climbing practices: belaying and sport leading.

The American Mountain Guides Association (AMGA) has established a rigorous curriculum and certification program for mountain guides. Guides achieve Rock, Alpine, and Ski certifications from the AMGA after thorough training, apprenticeship, and intense testing. The AMGA also certifies instructors of traditional climbing through its Single Pitch Instructor (SPI) program. But lots of other institutions that teach climbing—regional clubs, course providers like NOLS and Outward Bound, gyms, colleges and universities, summer camps, YMCAs, and scout troops—are not likely to send their staff through AMGA programs to achieve full guide certification. As a result, outside of the guiding world, there is an educational gap—every institution creates and teaches to its own safety standards. While many of these standards are exceptional, not all of them are. And even the exceptional ones are not consistent.

The AAC has begun working with many of these institutions to help unify them under a more universal standard. Since the AAC is our nation's sole representative of the International Climbing and Mountaineering Federation (UIAA), moving to a standardized training program has numerous benefits beyond just making our climbing world a safer place. A UIAA-approved certification for instructors and leaders who teach belaying and sport climbing—at various levels—would give educators a credential recognized around the world, much as the AMGA's Single Pitch Instructor course does for trad climbing. More importantly, these educators could deliver a consistent curriculum, giving our community a way to identify climbing partners who know their stuff, much as a Level 1 avalanche course does within the backcountry skiing world.

Wouldn't you like to be certain that your belayer learned from someone who "knows the ropes?" I know I would.

STERLING™

SECURITY

Sterling is proud to be the Founding Sponsor of American Alpine Club's "Know the Ropes" Gym to Crag Outdoor Initiative. We will continue to support the education and advocacy efforts of the AAC for the betterment of all who seek to enjoy the outdoors.

sterlingrope.com

Made in Maine | with U.S. & Globally-sourced Material.

RESCUE COVERAGE

Since 1948, the American Alpine Club has published *Accidents in North American Mountaineering* annually, helping you prevent accidents on your own. But prevention isn't the only answer for coming out of a crisis alive.

Even when using great judgment, no one is immune to accidents. Whether you're close to home or climbing on a faraway expedition, AAC rescue coverage provides peace of mind in case something goes wrong.

Members of the American Alpine Club are automatically enrolled for $10,000 of rescue benefits that pay for out-of-pocket costs in the United States as well as Global Rescue services internationally. These services get used regularly.

> "IN 2014 ALONE, 27 AMERICAN ALPINE CLUB MEMBERS WERE RESCUED ACROSS THE GLOBE."

COVERAGE

GLOBAL RESCUE ($5,000)

This benefit covers you anywhere in the world for rescue and evacuation by or under the direction of Global Rescue personnel. If you're injured beyond the trailhead, no matter the elevation, we will come to your aid. Members who want more than $5,000 of coverage can upgrade at a 5% discount by visiting americanalpineclub.org/rescue. *TO USE THIS BENEFIT:* Call +1 (617) 459-4200 as soon as possible during an emergency.

DOMESTIC RESCUE ($5,000)

This benefit reimburses AAC members for out-of-pocket rescue costs in the United States. This benefit can be used in addition to the Global Rescue service. *TO USE THIS BENEFIT*: File a claim within 30 days of evacuation by calling *(303) 384-0110* or emailing *claims@americanalpineclub.org*. We will send you a check.

ACTIVITIES COVERED

Climbing, hiking, backcountry skiing, mountain biking and more—if it's human-powered on land and you're rescued, you're covered as long as you're an active member.

JOIN THE AMERICAN ALPINE CLUB

Only active members of the AAC may use these services. To join, visit *www.americanalpineclub.org/join* or call *(303) 384-0110*. You will gain access to $10,000 of rescue coverage as soon as you pay dues. As a member you also will be supporting the publication of this book, and you'll receive free copies of the latest *Accidents in North American Mountaineering* and *American Alpine Journal*, among many other benefits.

Don't leave yourself hanging.

$10,000 COVERAGE WITH MEMBERSHIP.

americanalpineclub.org/rescue

KNOW THE ROPES
PROTECTION

BY RON FUNDERBURKE & KARSTEN DELAP //
PHOTOS BY DOUGALD MACDONALD & ERIK RIEGER

Along with a rope, protection is the most essential part of the climbing system. A bolt and quickdraw, a cam or nut—these are the things that keep climbers from taking dangerous ledge falls or hitting the ground. While not the most common cause of incidents reported in *Accidents*, failures of a lead climber's protection system occur frequently.

In 2012, for example, *Accidents* recorded data on 11 incidents where protection pulling out was the immediate cause of an accident. Placing no protection or inadequate protection were contributory causes for 27 accidents. Similar numbers were reported in 2013. So the lead climber's protection system, or lack thereof, is clearly worthy of consideration as climbers strive to be more skilled, more prudent, and less accident-prone.

While many climbs present rock features that cannot be adequately protected, the vast majority of failures of the protection system do not happen on such routes. As accident statistics continue to demonstrate, an error in judgment, a misunderstanding of protection systems, or lack of technical prowess are more often to blame when the protection system fails in some way.

In this installment of Know the Ropes, we will present perspectives and concepts designed to consolidate best practices in the implementation, evaluation, and reliance upon a lead climber's protection. We will cover the two main genres of rock climbing: sport climbing and traditional climbing.

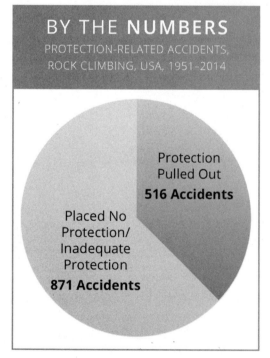

BY THE NUMBERS
PROTECTION-RELATED ACCIDENTS,
ROCK CLIMBING, USA, 1951–2014

Protection
Pulled Out
516 Accidents

Placed No
Protection/
Inadequate
Protection
871 Accidents

SPORT CLIMBING

While sport climbing is not the most easily categorized genre in climbing, we will rely on this definition: On sport climbs the entire protection system involves bolts and quickdraws; all bolts adequately protect the lead climber from ground or ledge falls (except in cases of human error); and the anchor components are fixed and permanent.

Sport climbing was created to optimize physical and athletic difficulty by de-emphasizing equipment challenges. Since the lead climber does not need to evaluate the rock, place his or her own gear, or make choices about the frequency and position of those placements, how is that accidents still occur? What kinds of protection-related best practices could reduce the number of sport climbing accidents?

CLIP QUICKDRAWS CORRECTLY

When a leader climbs up to a quickdraw and connects the climbing rope, there are two main variables: (1) where the leader's body is positioned on the climb relative to the quickdraw, and (2) how the climbing rope interacts with the carabiner being clipped.

The first variable is easy to imagine. If the lead climber falls before he/she can successfully clip a quickdraw, the fall length will be shorter if the quickdraw is at the leader's waist or chest level. If the lead climber reaches overhead to clip the rope into a quickdraw, extra slack will be needed, thereby increasing the fall length if the leader fails to make the clip. Often, doing one more move to reach a good hold will make for an easier clip and less rope to pull up. If this is imprudent or impracticable, the lead climber

[Top] The lead climber is stretching to clip overhead. Unless the clipping stance is very good, this generally isn't recommended because the extra rope can make for a big fall if the climber slips while clipping. [Bottom] It's often best to clip at waist or chest level. This uses less energy and results in less slack in the rope system should the climber fall while clipping.

should be hyper-vigilant and careful when clipping overhead.

If the leader finds he or she can't reach a good clipping hold or must clip from an out-of-balance stance, two temporary measures may be useful:

(1) Use a "stiff draw," in which a stick or other stiffener is taped to the quickdraw so it can be grasped low on the draw, giving the leader a few extra inches for clipping out-of-reach bolts.

(2) Clip a quickdraw to a distant bolt and then extend it with one or two additional draws clipped to the first. This allows the leader to clip the rope without pulling up additional slack. For redpoint attempts, a longer draw or sling can be left in place.

In both of these cases, the leader should place a normal quickdraw on the bolt and clip the rope to it as soon as he or she reaches a better stance.

The second important variable in clipping is found in the simple connection between a climber's rope and a bolt. Common errors include backclipping, gate interference, and carabiner leverage. To avoid all of these errors it is important to remember a few critical concepts.

First, the lead climber's rope should always travel along the plane of the rock, enter a carabiner from the rock side of the carabiner, and connect to the climber on his/her side of the carabiner's plane. If the rope is "backclipped" [see photos on

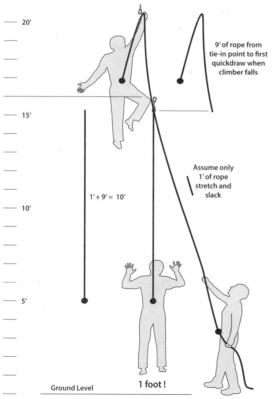

- 20'
- 15'
- 10'
- 5'

9' of rope from tie-in point to first quickdraw when climber falls

1' + 9' = 10'

Assume only 1' of rope stretch and slack

Ground Level   1 foot!

[Left] This illustration shows what can happen if the leader falls while clipping an overhead bolt. Though clipped into a bolt 16 feet up, he stops only one foot above the ground; with additional slack or rope stretch his feet easily could hit the ground. *Rick Weber* [Right] Use a "stiff draw" for out-of-reach bolts.

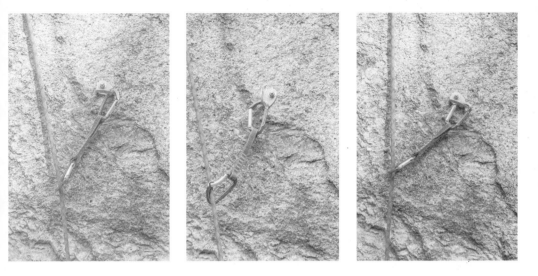

[Left] A properly clipped quickdraw, where the rope enters the carabiner from the rock side and exits on the climber's side. Ideally, the carabiner gates should be oriented opposite the direction of travel. [Middle] An incorrectly "backclipped" quickdraw. In a fall, a backclipped draw can come unclipped. [Right] Be careful in scenarios such as this, where the upward motion of the rope could cause the carabiner gate to press against the bolt hanger and unclip. Orienting both carabiners on the quickdraw in the same direction can help mitigate this issue.

p.15] it can unclip itself from the carabiner when the rope runs over the gate during a leader fall.

Second, a quickdraw should be clipped to a bolt so that the carabiner gates are oriented away from potential interference from rock features like knobs or other protrusions.

Third, to mitigate the risks of a carabiner coming unclipped from either the bolt or the rope, it's important to assemble your quickdraws so that both carabiner gates are oriented in same direction. The quickdraw always should be clipped to a bolt so that the gates of the carabiners are oriented in the opposite direction from the leader's anticipated direction of travel. This helps to prevent the rope from rubbing over the gate or pressing against the carabiner's gate in the event of a fall, potentially unclipping. This also helps prevent the lead climber's motion and the corresponding rope action from levering the carabiner gate against the bolt hanger, possibly causing it to unclip [see photos above].

Here's an example: If a climber is ascending a corner and all the bolts are on the left wall, which way should the gates on the quickdraws face? Answer: All the gates should face to the left, away from the climber.

Be cognizant of the different ways the lead climber's rope and body movements can jostle and alter a carabiner's position. In the case of a bolt, for example, a quick upward movement can cause a carabiner to load horizontally, backclip from the bolt, or be levered by the bolt hanger. Take a quick look at the draw after you move past it to make sure you didn't move it into a dangerous position.

If a route causes unusual concern about quickdraws unclipping, assemble a quickdraw with one or two small locking carabiners. Some climbers like to use a quickdraw with locking carabiners on the first bolt of every sport climb—or the first bolt above a ledge.

Finally, even though most sport routes are intended to be climbed without supplemental protection, in some cases placing an additional piece can prevent dangerous run-outs—or simply ease the mind. Check the guidebook for gear recommendations—does it suggest a particular nut or cam?

BEST PRACTICES: CLIPPING

- ASSEMBLE QUICKDRAWS CORRECTLY.
- CLIP QUICKDRAWS AT WAIST OR CHEST LEVEL WHEN POSSIBLE.
- AVOID BACKCLIPPING.
- BE SURE THAT CARABINER GATES POINT AWAY FROM POTENTIAL INTERFERENCE FROM BOLT HANGERS, ROCK FEATURES, OR ROPE ACTION.

USE RELIABLE BOLTS

Bolts can fail for a number of reasons. Maybe they were placed improperly, they could be past their useful life, the rock around them could be compromised, or they could be corroded. While it is tempting to regard bolts as "bomber" protection, all climbers should consider the blind faith they place in these critical links.

Since the developer of a given route is usually not on hand to ask directly, how should lead climbers evaluate a bolt's integrity? There are three main clues: corrosion, the rigidity of the bolt stud, and the tightness of the hanger.

Many bolts were not designed to be used in an outdoor setting, and extensive visible corrosion should be an immediate warning for a lead climber. Bolts also may be corroded inside the rock with no visible damage. Corrosion is especially common in marine settings (like seaside cliffs), wet or humid venues, or bolts placed in consistent seeps or drainages; climbers should be particularly vigilant in these environments.

If the bolt stud moves up and down, pulls in or out, or if it has visibly damaged the surrounding rock, due to leverage, there is clearly a problem. A quick outward pull on the hanger will usually reveal these weaknesses.

Spinning hangers can be a sign that something is not quite right with the bolt. It is possible a hanger is spinning because the bolt stud has pulled out of the rock slightly. Or a hanger might be spinning because the nut that is supposed to be pinning it against the rock has loosened. In either case, a quick test of the bolt stud, with an outward and side-to-side pull, will suggest whether there is a real hazard. Nuts that have simply loosened from continuous use should be tightened; a slight turn of a wrench should do the trick—the nut should be snug but not over-tightened.

If you suspect a bad protection or anchor bolt, never rely on that bolt alone. Back it up, if possible, or downclimb to better protection before retreating. (Leave a carabiner/quickdraw on a good bolt and lower to the ground.) If you spot a bad bolt and don't have the tools or expertise to fix it yourself, let the local community know with a note or online post.

AVOID WORN OR DEFECTIVE CARABINERS

Through repeated use, carabiners eventually become worn and grooved. Deeper grooves create sharper edges, and particularly sharp edges can knife the sheath off a climbing rope or sever it altogether. Similarly, repeatedly clipping an aluminum carabiner to a steel bolt or cable can cause burrs, abrasions, and rough teeth on the carabiner's otherwise smooth surface. Much like any serrated material, these burrs can seriously damage a climbing rope.

With the increasing popularity of pre-hung draws on sport climbing projects (this includes chain, cable, and nylon quickdraws), more ropes are being cut by carabiners that have been worn and have sharp edges. For example, in 2010, in the Red River Gorge, a leader clipped his rope into a quickdraw that had been left earlier on the first bolt of a difficult route. When the leader fell before the second bolt, his rope severed on the badly worn carabiner in the fixed draw and he hit the ground, suffering head injuries. While technology continues to make carabiners lighter, this can also cause them to wear faster.

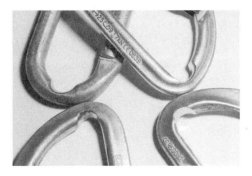

Ideally, every carabiner in the protection system should be carefully inspected before use, though this is not · always practical (especially when attempting onsights). Yet some

[Above] Deeply grooved carabiners. Replace any carabiners that look like this. *Black Diamond*

climbers still blindly head up every route assuming the fixed gear is in good condition. While the send is important, it is not as important as making sure the equipment is in good shape.

It is advisable for lead climbers to always hang their own quickdraw on the first bolt of a sport climb equipped with "perma-draws." The angle between the first quickdraw and the belayer tends to sharpen the carabiner on a permanent quickdraw here much faster than the carabiners higher on the route. If the first bolt is left empty as a standard practice, much of the deep grooving caused by the rope can be avoided, or at least concentrated on the leader's personal quickdraws. This also makes for easier stick-clipping.

Additionally, any fixed nylon quickdraws should be considered suspect unless you know their history. Damage from UV radiation can degrade nylon and cause the dogbone on a quickdraw to fail.

Burrs and grooves on carabiners are not only problematic with fixed draws but with your personal quickdraws as well. For example, bolts can cause abrasions in the carabiner's aluminum frame that can shred a climbing rope. To reduce this risk, dedicate one carabiner on each draw to clipping the bolt and one to clipping the rope.

BEST PRACTICES: CARABINERS

- RETIRE CARABINERS THAT ARE DEEPLY GROOVED, SCRATCHED, OR BURRED.
- WHEN USING QUICKDRAWS, DEDICATE ONE CARABINER TO CLIPPING THE BOLT AND THE OTHER TO CLIPPING THE ROPE.
- BEFORE USING A CARABINER, PREHUNG OR OTHERWISE, MAKE A QUICK VISUAL INSPECTION. IF A CARABINER IS WORN, YOU SHOULD BE ABLE TO "TAKE" ON THE DRAW AND THEN REPLACE IT. IF NOT, DOWNCLIMB TO THE NEXT LOWER DRAW AND RETREAT FROM THERE.
- ALWAYS USE YOUR OWN QUICKDRAW ON THE FIRST BOLT OF A SPORT CLIMB.

[Above] A variety of tools can be used to stick-clip the first bolt of a route. Make sure you do not backclip the draw.

AVOID UNNECESSARY RISKS

Stick-clipping the first or even the second bolt of a route is a great way to prevent a ground fall. If the first bolt is 15 feet off the ground, the next bolt should be no more than 5 feet higher if it is going to protect a leader from ground fall, given rope stretch and displacement of the belayer as he or she catches the fall. But many sport routes do not adequately protect a leader from ground fall in the first 20 feet. If they haven't stick-clipped, lead climbers then have to make a personal choice about whether to proceed. Too often, climbers rely entirely on their own ability to get them out of trouble. When a hold breaks or moves prove to be harder than predicted, it is too late to make an informed decision.

Sometimes, when the main difficulties of a sport climb have passed, lead climbers will confidently saunter into ground-fall or ledge-fall terrain, eschewing protection along the way. Skipping bolts and taking victory whippers are two common examples of unnecessary risks.

BEST PRACTICES: AVOIDING RISK

- STICK-CLIP THE FIRST BOLT WITH YOUR OWN QUICKDRAW IF THE CLIMBING TO THE FIRST BOLT IS DIFFICULT, LOOSE ROCK IS PRESENT, OR A GROUND FALL LIKELY WOULD CAUSE INJURY. IN SOME CASES, STICK-CLIPPING THE SECOND BOLT IS ADVISABLE.
- CLIP EVERY BOLT ON THE ROUTE TO AVOID GROUND OR LEDGE IMPACT.
- AVOID UNNECESSARY RUN-OUTS AND FALLS.

TRADITIONAL CLIMBING

Every protection failure that can occur in sport climbing can also occur in traditional climbing. A climber should be just as concerned about faulty equipment, clipping hazards, fixed hardware, and making informed choices in a traditional environment as at a sport crag. Moreover, traditional climbing involves vastly more variables, decision-making, and risk management. Creating and managing the protection system in traditional climbing takes expertise, craft, and artistry. Sadly, failures of the protection system usually result from human error.

In this section, we will discuss some important factors in creating a reliable protection system. We will discuss the placement decisions that result from an understanding of rock quality. Lastly, we will discuss fixed gear and route selection.

PROTECTING THE PITCH

Protecting the pitch is a term that is thrown around a lot, but what a climber is actually doing is creating an integrated protection system. For example, most climbers understand that the terrain before the first piece of protection has an unavoidable ground-fall consequence. From the first piece on upward, the lead climber is creating an integrated protection system that is supposed to mitigate the risk of ground fall, ledge impact, or other incidental impacts (hitting a slab, swinging

[Right] In this composite image, the climber has placed protection at 10-foot intervals yet is risking a ground or ledge fall throughout the first 30 feet of the climb. Place protection early, often, and at cruxes to avoid ground falls or unnecessarily long falls.

[Left] Nuts are often not a good choice for the first pieces of protection on a pitch. **[Middle]** As soon as tension is applied to the rope (for example, a fall) the nuts can be lifted up and out of constrictions, causing the protection to "zipper." **[Right]** A cam is a good choice for the first piece since it can sustain upward pulls and prevent other protection from pulling out.

into a corner, etc.). Unfortunately, lead climbers often climb into ground-fall terrain again before placing their second piece, or fail to protect sections altogether if the climbing feels fairly easy.

As in sport climbing, if you place a piece of gear 12 feet off the ground, your next piece must be no more than 4 feet above this to avoid a potential ground fall. (This is also true of any protruding terrain features like ledges.) Once you are well above the ground you can start to space gear farther apart, but it is prudent to always have a couple of pieces keeping you off the ground in case one fails. (If you find yourself with less than optimal protection, doubling up a placement is a good way to work some redundancy into the system.) In general, climbers should consider the consequences of going more than 10 feet between protection placements—falls of 20 feet or more may easily generate the kinds of forces that can seriously injure a climber, especially on less-than-vertical terrain.

Special consideration must be given to the first piece of gear. It should be able to hold an upward force as well as downward force to prevent zippering. Zippering is when multiple pieces of protection pull out as the rope impacts them in a fall—protection may zipper downward or upward. Depending on the angle between the belayer and the first piece, upward force may be generated when a fall happens and the first piece can be yanked up and out. In some cases, the subsequent pieces may fail in succession due to a similar angle in the rope. [See photos above.] In severe cases, it is possible that the only piece left would be the one that the climber fell onto, thereby reducing the entire protection system to a single piece of protection. Thankfully, most modern cams are designed for multidirectional pulls. They make excellent choices for the leader's first piece.

BEST PRACTICES: **THE PROTECTION SYSTEM**

- PLACE ENOUGH PROTECTION TO ADEQUATELY SAFEGUARD THE LEADER FROM GROUND FALL, LEDGE IMPACT, PENDULUM SWINGS, AND FALLS GREATER THAN 20 FEET.
- MAKE SURE THE FIRST PIECE OF PROTECTION CAN SUSTAIN AN UPWARD PULL. USUALLY, A CAM IS BETTER THAN A NUT.

PLACING PROTECTION

It would be impossible in an article of this length to fully discuss the placement of removable protection. Suffice to say, all removable protection generally relies on the same principles. When protection fails, it is almost always because one or more of those principles was ignored, overlooked, or misinterpreted. Removable protection requires sound rock quality (discussed later), security and stability, optimal surface contact between the piece and the rock, and an orientation that anticipates the loads that will be applied to it. Trad climbing is full of delightful trickery, but efficient leaders recognize that square pegs pretty much go in square holes.

Orientation: Cams, nuts, tricams, and hexes should all be placed in ways that anticipate the loads that will be applied to them. Nuts should be placed in constrictions in the rock that point downward. Cam stems should point toward the fall line. Hexes and tricams should lever along the fall line. Make no mistake, a lead fall will load the top piece of a protection system along the fall line, so it should be placed accordingly.

[Left] Don't place protection perpendicular to the rock plane. A fall can cause the protection to rotate and pull out. [Middle] Instead, place protection so that it anticipates the fall line. [Right] Nuts are best placed in downward-facing constrictions.

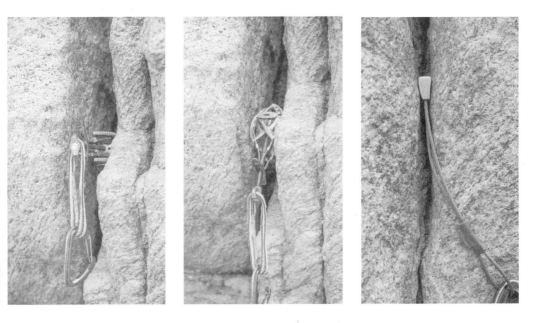

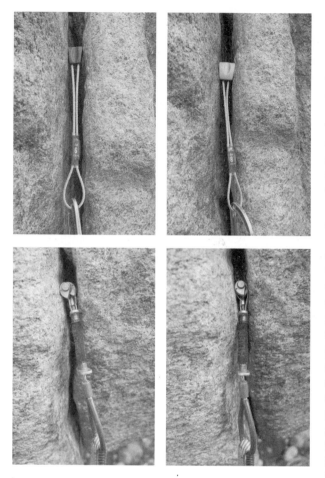

[Top, left] This nut does not have adequate surface contact on all sides and can pull out or fail. [Top, right] A slightly lower placement yielded a good constriction with optimal surface contact on the sides of the nut. [Bottom, left] The two upper cam lobes are not engaged with the rock. [Bottom, right] Moving the cam down resulted in a secure placement with all four lobes engaged.

Security and Stabilty: Once a piece of protection is placed, a variety of forces interact with that placement. Some of those forces can alter the orientation and quality of the placement. The rope, drawing through a carabiner, can swing a placement back and forth. In the case of cams, this side-to-side action can cause cams to "walk" out of their optimal placement. If the swinging motion of the rope creates an outward pull on nuts, hexes, or tricams, they can be lifted out of their constrictions. Managing the path the rope follows is essential if cam and nut placements are to be secure.

An appropriate length of extension (usually a long quickdraw or standard 24-inch or 48-inch nylon/dyneema sling) usually can mitigate this problem, because rope action tends to interact directly with the sling, instead of the placement. Another common tactic with nuts, hexes, and tricams is to give a light tug on the placement, thereby mashing the aluminum unit into the rock slightly. (Tugging too hard can make the unit difficult to remove, however.) Lastly, try to place cams in parallel features where you don't anticipate they can walk.

Square Pegs in Square Holes: It is vital, in terms of efficiency and effectiveness, to place protection in the most obvious ways, in order to optimize the amount of surface contact between the unit and the rock, to make timely choices and placements, and to get the most potential holding power and security. For example, all trad leaders should think of placing a cam when they attempt to protect a parallel feature in the rock. They should think of placing a nut or hex when they see a constriction, and they should think of placing a tricam in oddly shaped pods, pockets, or flares. Cams should be placed within their camming range. Nuts and hexes should have surface contact on all sides of the unit. Tricams should be placed and set within their rotational range.

Clearly, there are ways to make any trad piece work in almost any placement, given enough inventiveness. But, when trad leaders resort to putting square pegs in round holes, it should be for unique and demanding reasons, and there should be an understanding of the risks and time cost of these choices. Trad trickery can be an incredible waste of time—and dangerous—if it is indulged too whimsically.

It should be needless to say that if gear is so tattered by use and abuse that one can no longer tell if the pegs are round or square, the gear should be retired. When cam slings become visibly damaged or decomposed, they should be replaced. (A professionally sewn replacement sling is an option.) Similarly, frayed trigger wires, nut cables, and hex cables should be replaced with appropriately strong cord or webbing.

BEST PRACTICES: PLACING GEAR

- PLACE CAMS IN PARALLEL CRACKS, NUTS AND HEXES IN CONSTRICTIONS, AND TRICAMS IN PODS, POCKETS, AND FLARES, UNLESS NECESSITY DICTATES OTHERWISE. PUT SQUARE PEGS IN SQUARE HOLES.
- MAKE SURE PLACEMENTS ARE STABLE AND SECURE BY SETTING THEM (GIVE A QUICK DOWNWARD TUG), MANAGING THE ROPE LINE, AND USING EXTENSIONS APPROPRIATELY.
- PLACE EQUIPMENT IN AN ORIENTATION THAT ANTICIPATES THE LOAD THAT WILL BE APPLIED IN THE EVENT OF A LEAD FALL.

FIXED GEAR

Many traditional climbs are replete with abandoned nuts and cams, pitons, and aid climbing gear such as copperheads. These can be efficient to clip, but there can be great hazard in using them as well. Leaders always should be suspicious of fixed gear. Some fixed protection can be visually inspected, but, as with bolts, the key components of fixed gear may be obscured or buried. Imagine the wire on a nut that has rusted completely through, a sling that is mostly cut, the axle of the cam that is broken, or a piton that has completely decomposed or destroyed the rock around it. It is wise to back up fixed gear whenever possible.

Pitons are a remnant of the past in most rock climbing venues but are still placed infrequently in the alpine arena. Pins should be considered no good unless they can be tested with a hammer, which most free climbers don't carry. Pins can degrade behind the surface but still present a good-looking piece. Any corrosion on the pin can be an indication of corrosion deeper in the placement. Is the piton eye bent or cracked? Is there is any movement up and down? Does it wiggle side to side? Back up pins whenever possible.

BEST PRACTICES: FIXED GEAR

- INSPECT ALL FIXED GEAR CAREFULLY BEFORE USE.
- REMOVE DANGEROUS FIXED GEAR.
- BACK UP OLD OR SUSPICIOUS FIXED GEAR WITH OTHER PLACEMENTS.

[Top] In this scenario the protection is not adequately extended, causing the rope to bend and the protection to "walk." [Bottom] A long sling and quickdraw have been added to the pieces to straighten the rope path and reduce tugging on the protection.

MANAGING THE ROPE LINE

Unlike sport climbs, protection for traditional climbs may be placed along a wandering crack or other line of weakness, a traverse, a series of overhangs, or other variable features. As a result, keeping the rope running in a straight line is often an intricate challenge. A traditional lead climber should understand that excessive rope drag not only encumbers the leader's movement, it also decreases the dynamic properties of the protection system, thereby increasing potential impact forces on the protection and the lead climber.

A simple assortment of quickdraws will not suffice. Instead, lead climbers must use a variety of tactics to keep the rope running as straight as possible: placing slings of various lengths; possibly climbing with more than one lead rope; and sometimes downclimbing to remove lower protection once a good piece is placed higher up.

A lead climber should also understand that every sling or extension comes with a consequence: If the distance between the protection point and the attachment of the rope increases, the fall distance increases too. Prudent leaders learn to extend only when necessary to straighten the rope line—and only as far as necessary.

BEST PRACTICES: THE ROPE LINE

- CLIMB WITH ENOUGH SLINGS, CARABINERS, AND QUICKDRAWS TO PREVENT EXCESSIVE ROPE DRAG.
- EXTEND WHEN NECESSARY, BUT ONLY WHEN NECESSARY AND ONLY AS FAR AS NECESSARY.
- IF PROTECTION SYSTEMS WANDER EXTENSIVELY FROM SIDE TO SIDE, USE LESS COMMON ROPE-MANAGEMENT TECHNIQUES LIKE DOUBLE ROPE SYSTEMS.

ROCK QUALITY

Evaluating the rock is at least as important as knowing how to place gear in it. Often, lead climbers are simply trying to get up a pitch and don't always use all of their senses. Take a look at the rock, first at the big picture and then narrowing to the micro setting. Is this a solid crack or a flake of rock sitting on top of another rock? Can you see debris, ice, or vegetation inside the rock? Look at everything.

Next, how does the rock sound? Using a larger cam or nut to bang around the rock can help determine if a rock is loose, hollow, or perfectly

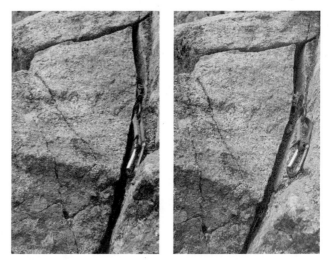

[Photos] Climbers should be wary of cracks formed by loose blocks such as this. A quick tug drastically expanded this placement.

solid. (An open palm or door-knocking motion also works.) The rock provides valuable clues about the viability of a placement. Is it loose? Crumbly? Slimy? Icy or wet? Try to use as many senses as possible to create a complete portrait.

When a leader must resort to placing gear in less than ideal rock, passive gear may create less prying forces on the rock than cams will; passive placements also may be more secure in flakes or jumbled boulders. Look around for other options. A solid placement off to the side of the route—with appropriate extension—may offer better protection than a placement in poor rock directly on the line. In softer rock (desert sandstone, for example), the leader should place pieces closer together to minimize fall forces. Double up on smaller pieces to decrease the odds of a catastrophic failure.

BEST PRACTICES: THE ROCK

- HAMMER ON POTENTIAL PLACEMENTS WITH A CAM, PALM, OR FIST TO GAIN INFORMATION ABOUT THE ROCK'S HOLLOWNESS, LOOSENESS, OR INSTABILITY.
- LOOK CLOSELY AT THE SURFACE THAT WILL MAKE CONTACT WITH PROTECTION TO AVOID CRUMBLY, SANDY, WET, OR ICY PLACEMENTS.
- DOUBLE UP ON PROTECTION PLACEMENTS IN SOFT OR SUSPECT ROCK.

ROUTE SELECTION

When we head out to the crag we should pick routes within our climbing ability, risk tolerance, and technical ability. For example, take the Original Route on Whitesides Mountain, North Carolina, which is rated 5.11a or 5.9 A0. If you are a 5.12 climber but are uncomfortable with long runouts or multi-pitch climbing, this may not be a good route for you. Any of the pitches could be considered "R-rated," and the first pitch, while only 5.7 slab, is mostly a free solo. However, if you are a solid 5.10 leader with extensive traditional climbing experience, and these pitches are within your risk tolerance, this can be a very manageable route.

To develop your skills as a leader, work up through styles and difficulties of routes to gain situational awareness. Reading topos and getting info from guidebooks and online resources also will help you pick an appropriate adventure and start the risk management process.

BEST PRACTICES: ROUTE SELECTION

- HOW LONG IS EACH PITCH AND HOW MANY PLACEMENTS CAN I EXPECT TO MAKE?
- ARE THERE CONTINUOUS CRACK SIZES THAT WILL REQUIRE MULTIPLE PLACEMENTS OF THE SAME SIZE?
- ARE THERE SPECIAL EQUIPMENT NEEDS, LIKE TRICAMS OR LARGE CAMMING UNITS?
- ARE THERE BOLTS ALONG THE WAY? HOW MANY? SHOULD I USE QUICKDRAWS OR EXTEND-ABLE SLINGS?
- ARE THERE PG-13, R, OR X RATINGS? DO I KNOW WHAT THAT MEANS? AM I COMFORTABLE WITH THAT?
- EVEN IF THE TERRAIN IS EASY, CAN I PROTECT MYSELF FROM AN UNLIKELY FALL?
- CAN I PLACE GEAR AT MY PHYSICAL (I.E., GRADE) LIMIT?

PUTTING IT ALL TOGETHER

If there is a theme that unites all of the strategies in this article, it is simply that informed decision-making is a huge part of safer climbing. Before a lead climber makes any move, there should be an understanding of the stakes of that move. What happens if a hold breaks? Where is my next protection? Given my strength and skill, what is the likelihood that I will make this move without falling? Stress, fatigue, social and performance pressures, and blind faith all are distracting, and these circumstances inhibit sound decision-making in any sport. But in climbing the consequences can be especially severe. While risk in climbing is inevitable, understanding and following the practices we've addressed in this article will mitigate that risk and prevent many accidents.

ABOUT THE AUTHORS

Ron Funderburke is an AMGA-certified Rock Guide and the Discipline Coordinator of the AMGA SPI (single-pitch instructor) program. He lives in Mills River, North Carolina, with his wife, Mary, and sons Burke and James.

Karsten Delap is an AMGA-certified Rock and Alpine Guide and co-owner of Fox Mountain Guides and Climbing School. He lives in Brevard, North Carolina, and guides rock and alpine routes throughout the United States.

THE NOSE

WHERE AND WHY ACCIDENTS OCCUR ON EL CAP'S
MOST POPULAR ROUTE // BY JOEL PEACH

The Nose of El Capitan began capturing people's attention well before the first ascent in 1958. Long, aesthetic, and immediately visible upon entering the Valley, it has all the makings of a classic line. At 5.9 C2, the Nose is considered to be the easiest full-length route on El Capitan, which makes it extremely popular and draws relatively inexperienced big-wall climbers. But the Nose also is a complex climb, requiring a large repertoire of techniques that may be unfamiliar to newcomers.

In the nearly 60 years since it was first climbed, the Nose has seen more than its share of accidents. We surveyed the last 41 years of incidents reported in *Accidents in North American Mountaineering* (1974–2014 publication dates). Of the 101 reports from El Capitan published during that time span, 41 (by far the largest concentration) covered incidents on the Nose, involving 44 separate parties.

The Nose is unusual for El Capitan because all of its bivouacs are on natural ledges and because there is a high percentage of free climbing on the route, compared with the steeper, blanker aid climbs to either side. (Only the Salathé Wall is similar in these ways.) Nevertheless, the most common accidents on the Nose, including leader falls, falling objects, and stranding in foul weather, are also common on other El Cap routes, and many of the lessons apply to other big-wall climbs, both in Yosemite Valley and elsewhere. Indeed, many of the accidents that happen on El Capitan are similar to those that occur on smaller crags, but the consequences are magnified by the scale of the cliff.

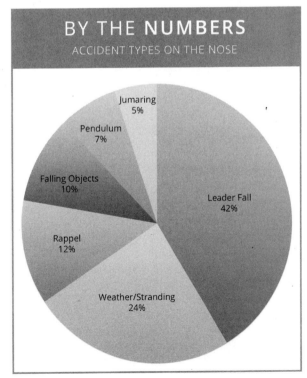

BY THE NUMBERS
ACCIDENT TYPES ON THE NOSE

- Jumaring 5%
- Pendulum 7%
- Falling Objects 10%
- Rappel 12%
- Weather/Stranding 24%
- Leader Fall 42%

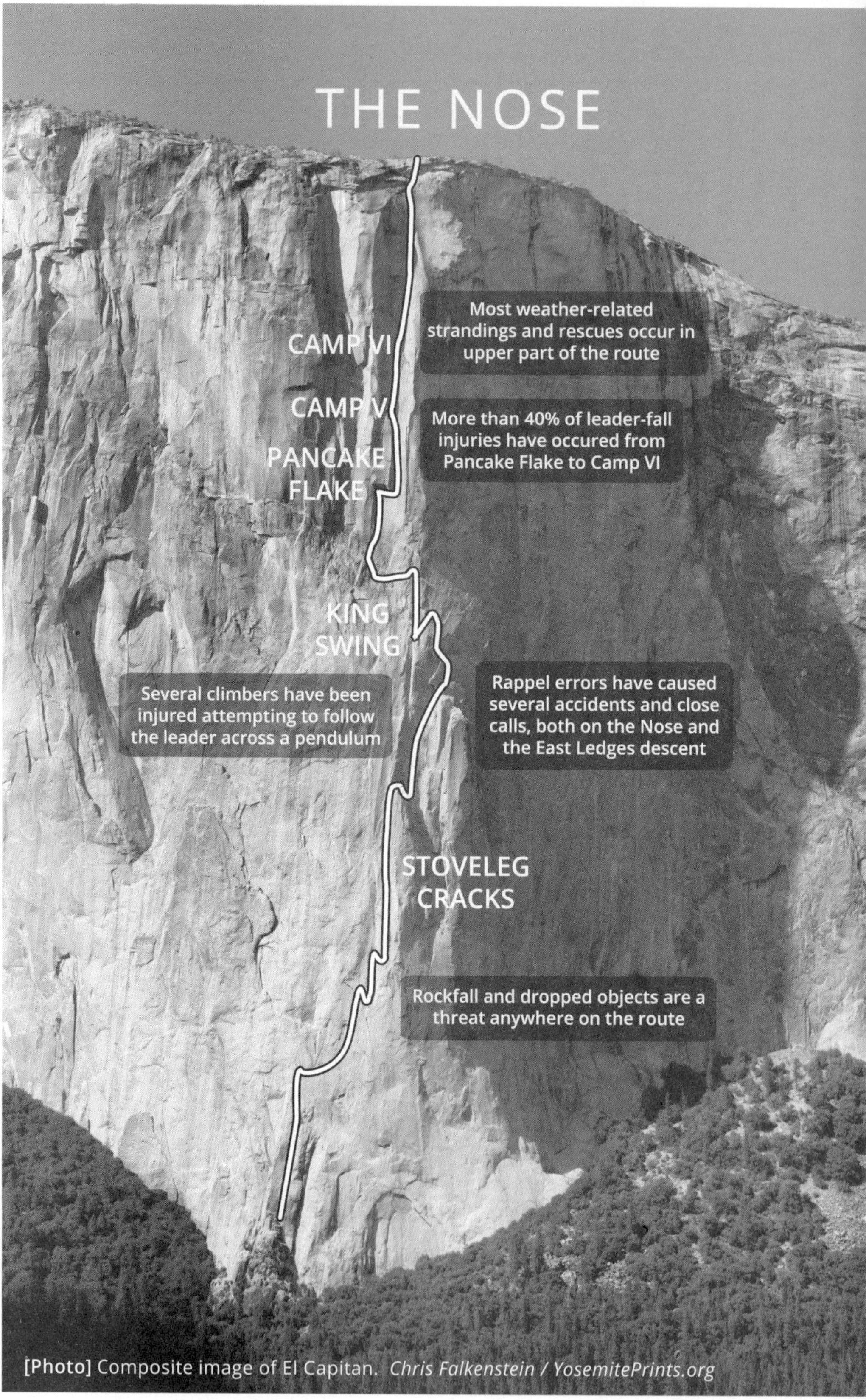

THE NOSE

CAMP VI

CAMP V

PANCAKE FLAKE

KING SWING

STOVELEG CRACKS

Most weather-related strandings and rescues occur in upper part of the route

More than 40% of leader-fall injuries have occured from Pancake Flake to Camp VI

Several climbers have been injured attempting to follow the leader across a pendulum

Rappel errors have caused several accidents and close calls, both on the Nose and the East Ledges descent

Rockfall and dropped objects are a threat anywhere on the route

[Photo] Composite image of El Capitan. *Chris Falkenstein / YosemitePrints.org*

The National Park Service does not require registration for climbing in Yosemite, so we are unable to say what percentage of all climbs of El Capitan end with these outcomes. Nonetheless, it is our hope we can call attention to the most common accidents and discuss what might be done to prevent future climbers on the Nose from appearing in these pages.

LEADER FALLS & PROTECTION

More than 40 percent of the incidents on the Nose reported in the pages of *Accidents* have involved leader falls. In most cases, the reports cited insufficient or poorly placed protection. In all cases but one, one or more pieces of protection pulled out. (The exception was a fatal incident in 1977 in which a climber temporarily clipped into a bight on a rope instead of tying in directly as he maneuvered to free a stuck rope. The rope then came unclipped when he fell.) While a few of the pieces of protection that pulled out were fixed, the majority had been placed while free climbing or aiding.

Among the reports involving a lead fall that referenced the climber's experience level, inexperience did *not* correlate to the likelihood of an accident. In other words, highly experienced climbers have injurious or fatal falls on the Nose—in some cases when they choose to run it out instead of placing sufficient pro.

Although the leader falls reported in these pages were spread along the full length of the wall, more than 40 percent of them happened along the pitches between Pancake Flake and Camp VI (pitches 23, 24, 25, or 26, depending on the individual report's pitch count for the route). The pitch directly above Camp V, leading to the Glowering Spot, has seen multiple accidents, in part because of the ledges that lie just below the harder climbing on this pitch. All of the incidents on this pitch occurred when an aid piece pulled out, suggesting the need for more practice with aid placements and movement before attempting the Nose. Generally, most leader-fall reports described one or more of the following subjective factors:

BACK-CLEANING

- "Although he carried three of each size of camming device...[he] felt he should back-clean...his protection."
- "He back-cleaned the other nut to get the quickdraw, because he felt he was running out of them and didn't want to disassemble the quickdraws on his cams."
- "He attributes the long fall to having back-cleaned a good piece, thinking he'd need it later."

INSUFFICIENT PROTECTION

- "[He] had placed no protection above the belay station bolts. He fell feet-first about 30 feet."
- "...so I skipped clipping the bolts and climbed higher."
- "Falling on the first pitch is a common occurrence. Not having adequate protection in this situation is the reason climbers fall to the deck."

CASCADING FAILURE

Where protection was placed, longer-than-expected falls almost always resulted from multiple pieces of gear failing:

- "[He]...was standing on a fixed wired nut when it broke. A small Friend he had placed pulled out during his fall."
- "At least two failed pieces, possibly fixed, contributed to his striking the ledge."
- "While standing on a TCU (#0 or #1), it popped from the crack. He also pulled the stopper below the TCU."

As with many big-wall routes, the recommended gear list for the Nose is extensive, including two to three sets of cams and nuts. Climbers may lighten their racks for a variety of reasons—and consequently may need to back-clean or run it out on a pitch—but doing so should always be balanced against the ability to protect pitches adequately. Moreover, as with plane crashes, falling itself is rarely problematic—it's the sudden impact with a ledge, flake, or corner that causes injury. Be aware of such obstacles before making the decision to back-clean or run it out.

Finally, consider how the rope is running through your protection and whether the pieces below you may be compromised when your rope suddenly goes taut in a fall. See "Know the Ropes" in this edition for more information on extending protection pieces to keep them from popping out in a fall.

WEATHER & BEING STRANDED

Veteran YOSAR ranger John Dill makes a succinct point about Yosemite Valley weather in his essential essay "Staying Alive" [see box below] by citing two incidents from the same date, just one year apart:

- On Oct. 11, 1983, a climber on El Cap collapsed from heat exhaustion.
- On Oct. 11, 1984, a party on Washington Column was immobilized by hypothermia.

Dill adds: "You can expect this range of weather year-round."

Weather was a major factor in a quarter of the incident reports for the Nose. Not only is the weather unpredictable year-to-year, as Dill points out, but storm systems can quickly and unexpectedly develop during the four to five days most parties spend on the Nose, especially (but not exclusively) during the popular fall season and winter.

It's worth noting that no weather-related incidents were reported in the first half of the climb. In all likelihood, the weather forecast was promising for the period the parties assumed it would take to summit, but then the weather went bad when they were higher up. Moreover, retreat is easier in the first half of the route than in the second half.

STAYING ALIVE

In addition to providing dozens of accident analyses for this publication over the years, longtime YOSAR ranger John Dill wrote "Staying Alive," an analysis of the Yosemite climbing accidents between 1970 and 1990. It is a trove of useful advice gleaned from decades of analyzing accidents (many on the Nose), and it should be considered essential reading for anyone considering their first El Cap route. You can find it in the Supertopo guidebook to El Capitan or at the Friends of Yosar website.

Amplifying the serious effects of unexpected foul weather is the topography of the route. Natural ledge camps coax climbers into leaving robust (but heavier) portaledges behind in favor of bivy sacks or tarps. And on the upper pitches, inclement weather often means impromptu waterfalls and water funneling down the cracks from rain or melting ice. The areas around Camp V and VI and above are particularly vulnerable to run-off.

When faced with impending storms, many climbers covered in *Accidents* chose to race the weather to the top rather than retreat. This is a dicey proposition since the higher pitches can ice over, and tired and possibly hypothermic climbers may struggle on the steep, strenuous upper pitches. In two separate incidents, climbers racing storms died on the last pitch of the route. Also, as one incident analysis pointed out, "The summit is only halfway to safety. Had [they] reached the top, they would have found themselves... facing deep snow, high wind, low visibility, and dangerous terrain."

At least one party of climbers involved in a weather-related incident

[**Above**] A serious storm hit these climbers atop El Cap Tower, eventually forcing a difficult retreat. *Gordon Wiltsie*

specifically had chosen the Nose because descent is possible from any pitch. However, when the situation became critical, they did not have the confidence to negotiate a retreat. In other cases, climbers had adequate gear and shelter to wait out a storm, but lacked sufficient food and water.

While the weather forecast might give guidance on whether and when to start an attempt, it shouldn't be construed as permission to neglect key areas of readiness. Shelter and clothing should be storm-ready and field-tested. Synthetic clothing and sleeping gear are essential. Parties should carry ample food and water to allow them to wait out poor conditions. Lastly, climbers should study retreat routes and carry the gear needed to make multiple rappels in serious weather.

ROCKFALL & FALLING OBJECTS

For some time, it has been considered unethical (and in Yosemite illegal) to jettison objects from a big-wall climb. In addition to the "ick factor" of a poo bag intentionally chucked from 1,500 feet, nearly any object dropped even half a pitch can present a serious threat to those climbing below.

[Above] The King Swing has been the site of several accidents. *Tom Evans / El Cap Report*

When rocks or flakes come loose, the results can be catastrophic. In 1988 there were two incidents in which falling blocks severed lead ropes. One party was "lucky" to escape with the belayer only suffering a broken arm. In the other case, the leader was already falling when a rock cut his rope and he fell nearly 2,000 feet to the Valley floor.

Smaller rocks (or carabiners, cams, water bottles, food containers, or any other object) can cause serious injuries. As described in a 1993 report, a climber ascending fixed lines to Sickle Ledge was sent to the medical clinic with head lacerations after being beaned with rocks dropped by other climbers already on the ledge.

Helmets are a must. But a helmet cannot protect climbers against large falling blocks. For the sake of climbers below, all climbers on El Capitan must take great care to avoid pulling off loose rocks when placing protection, managing the rope, and maneuvering around ledges or flakes. In addition, when possible, belayers should consider an anchor set-up that gives them a little freedom to dodge falling objects, as long as the set-up does not compromise the belay. Finally, during the weeks and months leading up to an ascent, climbers should stay up to date on the route by reading online trip reports and other updates that might mention hazardous flakes or loose blocks to avoid.

PENDULUMS

Three accidents reported in the past four decades involved pendulums (two on the King Swing and one on the pitch seven traverse to the crack leading to Dolt Hole). In all three cases, climbers underestimated their acceleration and collided with rock features, resulting in significant injury. [*Editor's note: Another King Swing accident took place in 2014. See page 52.*]

All three of these pendulum accidents involved a climber following the pitch, after the leader had successfully made the pendulum. Usually the second must lower himself out from the anchor he's leaving before starting a swing. It's easy to underestimate the amount one needs to lower before making a safe pendulum traverse. While most climbers have experience falling vertically, many fail to realize that swinging through a 90-degree arc can generate just as much speed—and at an angle that exposes vital organs to the impact. This suggests that seconds need to lower as far as they can with the extra rope they have available—or, quite likely, use a second rope to ensure an adequate lower-out.

DESCENT

The Nose is equipped to allow a rappel descent from any pitch of the climb. However, route-finding during the descent is crucial. In separate incidents, two parties became stranded after getting lost on the standard rappel route. One was able to continue once visibility improved. The other was unable to reascend and, having inadequate water, required a rescue.

Other cases involved the more typical difficulties and dangers of rappelling—perhaps amplified by exposure and the necessity for multiple rappels. One climber required assistance after a knot became stuck when rappelling, and another had a close call when an attempt to cut a T-shirt free from a belay device resulted in severed rappel ropes. One accident with multiple fatalities may have resulted in part from anchor failure.

Various El Capitan climbers have run into trouble on the standard East Ledges descent route from the summit, including one fatal accident. The East Ledges descent combines rappelling, downclimbing, and talus scrambling, at a time when climbers are likely tired and toting heavy haul bags. Despite one's understandable eagerness to return to the Valley floor, it may be safer and more relaxing to spend another night on the summit and do the descent in the morning.

In addition to studying the rappel route (and carrying a topo of the descent) in case it's necessary to bail from the climb, the fundamentals of safe rappelling—knotting the rope ends, using a friction backup, and double-checking each rappel set-up before unclipping from the anchor—must be followed when retreating from a big-wall climb. All the more so because retreat is likely happening when climbers are tired or stressed by poor weather.

FINAL WORD

Most of the accidents that happen on the Nose are the same types of accidents that happen elsewhere. Climbers succumb to objective hazards. They take falls and pull out protection. They get tired, overestimate their abilities, or make mistakes. A climb of this scale elevates not only the climber's ambition, but also the stakes, in a way that only 3,000 feet of towering granite can.

Search "El Capitan Accident History, 1973-2013" to find a complete table of El Capitan incidents reported in Accidents. The online version of this story (publications. americanalpineclub.org) will have a link to this table.

ALASKA

FALL ON SNOW | Climbing Unroped, Party Separated
DENALI, DENALI PASS

Sylvia Montag, 39, fell to her death on May 5 while attempting to descend from Denali Pass (18,200 feet) to the 17,200-foot high camp on the West Buttress Route. Montag had separated from her partner, Meik Fuchs, as they descended from Denali Pass, where they had camped for two nights in strong winds after an ascent of the Muldrow Glacier Route on the north side of the mountain.

Fuchs contacted the Talkeetna Ranger Station at 11 a.m. on May 5, asking for the lock combination to the rescue cache at the 17,200-foot camp, as he did not have adequate supplies without Montag, who was carrying their tent. He reported that Montag had turned around and decided to go back to Denali Pass, due to either fatigue or bad weather. NPS rangers in Talkeetna gave Fuchs the lock code and instructed him to build a camp. In high winds, he instead pulled gear out of the cache and used the cache box as a shelter.

At 10 a.m. on May 6, Talkeetna rangers were contacted by Augustin Bossart, a friend of Fuchs. Bossart requested a rescue for Fuchs and Montag, and reported that they had become separated, did not have adequate supplies, and that Fuchs had suffered frostbite on all 10 fingertips. Fuchs contacted Talkeetna an hour later with the same information and a request for rescue. Unflyable weather and a lack of nearby climbers or rangers prevented any rescue that day.

On the morning of May 7, weather above 12,000 feet had improved considerably, but a solid cloud layer between 6,000 and 10,000 feet prevented flights from Talkeetna into the range. However, an Air Force Rescue Hercules C-130 was able to overfly the entire upper mountain. The crew was able to locate cloud openings, but none was large enough to facilitate a helicopter rescue. The C-130 did not locate Montag, nor any sign of her near Denali Pass, during its flights from 9:15 a.m. to 4 p.m.

At approximately 4:45 p.m., a local air taxi radioed that weather had improved between 6,000 and 10,000 feet, and that the weather between Talkeetna and base camp was rapidly improving. Helicopter 3AE, with three rangers on board, departed Talkeetna and arrived at base camp at 6:30 p.m. Ranger Dave Weber then flew to Denali Pass and conducted a hasty search for Montag. Weber located Montag face-down, partially buried by snow, and deceased at 17,419 feet, about 800 feet directly below Denali Pass. With a lack of acclimatized rangers available, Talkeetna Incident Command decided to rescue Fuchs and return for Montag at a more opportune time. Fuchs was lifted from the 17,200-foot camp via short-haul rescue basket, unattended, and then assessed at base camp. Helicopter 3AE, three rangers, and Fuchs then flew to Talkeetna, where Fuchs was released from NPS care with minor frostbite. Significant bad weather prevented rangers from getting to high camp until May 22. On May 23, an NPS patrol led by Coley Gentzel was able to locate and extricate Montag's body, which was flown to Talkeetna for transfer to the Alaska medical examiner.

An interview with Fuchs shed some light on the events leading up to the fall. Notably, Fuchs reported that he had not actually seen Montag return to Denali Pass, but that he had assumed she returned to the pass. Based on this information and

DENALI PASS
(18,200')

APROX. START OF
MONTAG FALL

APROX. START OF
ROMANIAN FALL

HIGH CAMP (17,200')

[Above] More fatal falls occur along the "Autobahn," the traverse between high camp and Denali Pass, than any other part of the West Buttress Route. *NPS Photo*

where Montag came to rest, it is likely that Montag fell while descending. Fuchs also reported that at several points along their ascent route, he was surprised to find himself substantially faster than Montag. The pair had not previously climbed together, and Fuchs had assumed Montag to be the stronger and faster of the two; however, this did not prove to be true. Fuchs and Montag were roped together only on the Muldrow Glacier for crevasse protection. They did not travel roped on Karstens Ridge, the Harper Glacier, or while descending Denali Pass. [*Source: Denali National Park Case Incident Record and NPS press release.*]

ANALYSIS

According to Denali National Park, the so-called "Autobahn," the snow and ice slope between the 17,200-foot camp and Denali Pass, now has seen 12 fatalities—one of the most dangerous places on the mountain. Each season rangers and guide staff install fixed pickets, permanently equipped with quickdraws, along this slope. In the past they were placed every 30 to 35 meters, but the ranger staff plans to place more pickets, narrowing the gaps to about 27 meters, thus allowing a team with a 60-meter rope to be clipped into two pickets at any time. However, the pickets usually are not installed until the first ranger patrol or guided party reaches high camp, generally in mid-May. Moreover, pickets may be buried, removed, or fall out. In other words, climbers cannot assume the pickets will be in place. In this particular incident, the climbers had been moving unroped throughout their ascent and descent of the upper mountain. In such circumstances, even if they had stayed together, there is little Fuchs could have done to stop Montag's fall. Only a roped team placing protection or clipping fixed pickets is prepared to halt a fall on the Autobahn when self-arrest fails. [*Source: The Editors, with information on fixed protection policies provided by Coley Gentzel, Lead Mountaineering Ranger.*]

FALL ON SNOW | Inadequate Protection, Fatigue
DENALI, DENALI PASS

On May 10 four members of the Romanian team "Explorer Denali 2014" flew to the Kahiltna base camp to begin their climb. Over the following 13 days they progressed at an average rate up the West Buttress Route.

On May 23 three of the team members made their summit attempt, departing high camp at 9:45 a.m. High winds made for a challenging and long day, which continued into the early hours of May 24. Having completed 85 percent of the traverse back to high camp from Denali Pass, one of the climbers was preparing to clip into the final protection picket when she was pulled down the slope by the fall of one of her partners. After the fall, this climber was reported to be unconscious for approximately 30 minutes. Her two partners and another climbing team transported the injured climber back to high camp. At 2:30 a.m., guides from several companies established communication with ranger Dave Weber at the 14,200-foot camp and provided medical care.

The NPS rescue helicopter launched from Talkeetna at 5:37 a.m., picked up ranger Weber from the 14,200-foot camp, and proceeded to high camp. The patient was loaded onto the helicopter and flown to Talkeetna, where she was transferred to an air ambulance. She was assessed at the hospital and released the same day. [*Source: Denali National Park Case Incident Record.*]

[Below] "Fixed" picket prepared for the traverse to Denali Pass. *NPS Photo*

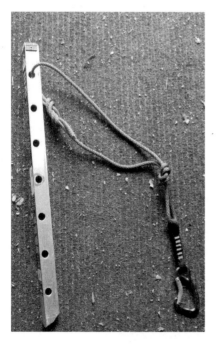

ANALYSIS

This team was roped up and using protection as they descended the Autobahn traverse, but they had not clipped sufficient protection to stop the entire team from sliding once one climber fell. After a very long summit day, it's likely that fatigue contributed significantly to the fall. [*Source: The Editors.*]

Editor's note: Guides Ben Adkison and Kyle Bates, both with Mountain Trip, received the 2014 Mislow-Swanson Denali Pro Award for their efforts and expertise in orchestrating the rescue of the critically injured Romanian climber. Adkison and Bates managed the patient's care for five hours in the middle of the night until daybreak, when National Park Service personnel could be flown to high camp. "Their professionalism allowed for a seamless and timely evacuation in the demanding mountain environment at 17,200 feet, and their extraordinary efforts resulted in a positive outcome for a severely injured patient," the award citation read.

FROSTBITE, ALTITUDE ILLNESS
DENALI, WEST BUTTRESS

On May 12 eight members of the military climbing team "U.S.M.C. Mtn. Warfare Training Center" flew to the Kahiltna Glacier to begin their climb. Over the following 12 days they progressed at an average rate up the West Buttress Route. On May 23, four of the team members departed for a summit attempt, reaching the top early on May 24. The party reported high winds and cold temps that contributed to their long push to the summit. The remaining four members of the team stayed in high camp to nurse varying levels of altitude illness.

The entire team of eight descended to the 14,200-foot camp during the afternoon of May 24 and immediately notified NPS personnel of a multitude of injuries and illnesses within their group. Following a brief triage of the climbers, it was determined that two warranted NPS medical assistance. One 25-year-old climber suffered from a variety of symptoms, including nausea, vomiting, dehydration, fatigue, headache, and profound weakness for multiple days. The second climber, 32, suffered partial- and full-thickness frostbite on all 10 toes and several fingers during his summit day. Both patients were stabilized and given recommendations for care during their descent. The two were re-evaluated on the morning of May 25 by NPS medical personnel before they continued down to the 7,200-foot base camp. They returned to Talkeetna on May 26 via their prearranged fixed-wing air taxi. [*Source: Denali National Park Case Incident Record.*]

ANALYSIS
Recognizing the serious weather conditions and heeding warning signs of altitude illness as these climbers ascended the upper mountain should have convinced them to halt their summit bid before it continued long into the night, which, in turn, likely exacerbated the frostbite injuries. See Denali ranger Dave Weber's short article on frostbite prevention, assessment, and treatment on the next page. [*Source: The Editors.*]

FALL ON SNOW, ALTITUDE SICKNESS | Party Separated
DENALI, DENALI PASS

On June 15, three European climbers from separate teams suffered varying degrees of frostbite, exposure, and minor injuries from falls while descending the upper mountain in poor weather.

At 12:30 a.m., climber Steve House contacted the NPS patrol led by ranger Brandon Latham at high camp and told rangers he had been helping a climber down the Autobahn (the descent from Denali Pass). The climber had taken two fairly substantial falls. After the second fall, which the climber self-arrested, House helped the climber anchor himself to a fixed picket, where he said he wanted to wait for other climbers who were higher on the mountain.

These other climbers eventually reached the injured climber and spent approximately four hours getting him down to a point four to five rope lengths above inconsequential terrain. A U.S. Army expedition helped lower the climber about three rope lengths. When ranger Latham's team arrived on scene, they conducted two more lowers to reach a litter positioned at the bottom of the Autobahn. Latham's team of three, plus six emergency-hired climbers from high camp, pulled the litter across the

ESSENTIALS
FROSTBITE

BY DAVE WEBER

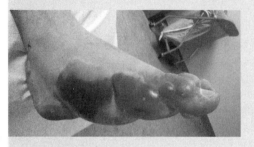

[Photo] Deep frostbite injury. *University of Utah Burn Center*

Frostbite is localized freezing of tissue that results in a range of signs, symptoms, and outcomes for alpinists. The areas farthest from the body core (fingers, toes, ears, nose, and genitals) are most commonly affected. Early recognition and subsequent rewarming are essential to minimizing the extent of tissue damage. The following recommendations are based on the Wilderness Medical Society's "Practice Guidelines for the Prevention and Treatment of Frostbite."

PREVENTION
Clothing must be sufficient to protect the climber from wind and cold. Clothing layers that get wet, either from overexertion or precipitation, should be changed out for dry layers as soon as practical. When tissue initially becomes cold and numb, alpinists should actively rewarm those areas before continuing their ascent/descent.

ASSESSMENT
Frostbite is commonly classified into two categories: superficial or deep. Rewarming of the affected tissue must be completed prior to evaluation of injury severity, as hallmark signs and symptoms can be masked when tissue is frozen. Superficial injuries tend to heal within the first month if not allowed to refreeze, while deep injury can result in ongoing pain and potentially permanent tissue loss. Each instance of frostbite will predispose a climber to increased risk for future frostbite injury.

SUPERFICIAL FROSTBITE *(Damage limited to the outermost layers of skin)*
· Numbness
· Blanching of skin (pale)
· Skin remains pliable
· Mild pain and swelling upon rewarming
· No immediate blister formation, but clear-fluid blistering is possible

DEEP FROSTBITE *(Inner and outer skin layers affected, with potential underlying muscle, tendon, and bone damage)*
· Significant diminishment of circulation, sensation, and motion
· Skin discoloration (red, purple, and/or black)
· Skin is frozen and non-pliable
· Intense pain and significant swelling upon rewarming is likely

- No immediate blister formation, but blood-filled blisters are likely
- Eschar (black, dead tissue) can develop over days/weeks following rewarming

FIELD TREATMENT

Patient should be removed from the cold environment and wet layers exchanged for dry. Hypothermia should be treated before any frostbite injury. Once hypothermia is managed, as long as there is no chance of the tissue refreezing, it should be thawed immediately, either by skin-to-skin rewarming or warm-water bath (99°–102°F, 37°–39°C), if available. Do not rub injured tissue—friction may cause additional damage. Do not allow frostbitten tissue to refreeze. Loose-fitting gauze, aloe vera, and ibuprofen should be used if available. Pain control may be required, especially with deep frostbite.

HOSPITAL TREATMENT

Advanced treatments now available at specialized centers offer improved chances of preserving tissue damaged by deep frostbite. Note that thrombolytic therapies (clot busting) require immediate patient evacuation—the elapsed time from thawing of frozen tissue to arrival at a burn/frostbite center must be no greater than 24 hours. Climbers or their physicians should contact local burn specialists or the University of Utah Burn Center (801-581-2700) for deep frostbite consultation and treatment.

Dave Weber is a Denali mountaineering ranger and lead medic, and flight paramedic for Intermountain Life Flight in Salt Lake City.

flats to reach the patient's tent. Two climbers were subsequently evacuated from high camp by NPS helicopter. [*Source: Denali National Park Case Incident Record.*]

ANALYSIS

Although it's not uncommon for climbers to ascend the upper West Buttress Route alone and/or unroped, these practices obviously are risky. In addition, the climbers that got into trouble this day clearly had overextended themselves—and perhaps underestimated the difficulties of an "easy" route like the West Buttress. Although climbers from Europe and the Lower 48 may have the necessary experience with glaciated mountains, Denali adds the substantial difficulties of higher altitude and extreme cold, for which some climbers are inadequately prepared. [*Source: The Editors.*]

FALL ON SNOW | Avalanche, Climbing Unroped

DENALI, WEST BUTTRESS

While waiting for stable weather to attempt a difficult route on Denali's south side, members of the New Zealand Alpine Team and friends climbed the West Buttress Direct, above Windy Corner, on June 13. The climbers had split into separate rope teams. Near the top of the ridge, the slope angle decreased and the upper team made the decision to continue unroped. One of the climbers had almost reached the top of the ridge, at approximately 16,000 feet, when he attempted to knock a snow mushroom off the side

[Left] A climber near the top of the West Buttress Direct on Denali, shortly before a small avalanche caused him to fall. [Right] The climber's fractured right leg. *Daniel Joll (both photos)*

of a rock outcrop. This triggered a small snow slide from above the outcrop, which pulled him off and sent him tumbling approximately 50 meters down the ice slope. He was seen trying to self-arrest, and he eventually came to a stop in a small depression with a broken right leg and other, minor injuries.

The fallen climber and his partners began a self-evacuation by rappels. Eventually they were joined by members of the other team, who helped with the rappelling efforts. The climbers descended more than 2,000 feet to reach the climbers' trail on the West Buttress Route, just above Windy Corner. Two climbers then traveled up to the 14,200-foot camp, and at approximately 7 p.m. they alerted the NPS ranger staff about the accident and requested assistance.

Ranger Brandon Latham and volunteers descended to the scene with medical supplies and a Cascade toboggan. Assessment revealed that the victim had an angulated right leg fracture and other injuries. He was packaged and transported uphill to the 14,200-foot medical tent, where he was stabilized. At 8 a.m. the following day he was evacuated by NPS helicopter to Talkeetna. [*Source: Denali National Park Case Incident Record.*]

ANALYSIS

Even small-scale avalanches can precipitate a fall, and climbing unroped increases the risk that a minor slip will turn into a major tumble. This climber was very fortunate that his fall did not continue all the way down the West Buttress. The team's efficient descent of more than 2,000 feet of steep, technical terrain with an injured partner was a commendable example of skilled self-rescue. [*Source: The Editors.*]

FALL ON SNOW
DENALI, WEST BUTTRESS

On June 29, Alpine Ascents International (ALP)-9 was descending the fixed ropes after a stay at the 17,200-foot camp. Toward the bottom of the fixed lines, at about 15,400 feet, one of the clients took a short twisting fall and heard a "click" in her right knee. She immediately felt a sharp pain. She was able to continue her descent by sliding in the deep snow and bracing her injured knee with her left leg.

After arriving at the 14,200-foot camp, ALP-9 guides Ben Jones and Peter Moore contacted NPS staff and requested a medical examination for their client. There were no significant findings beyond her knee injury. The guides were instructed to self-treat and allow time to heal.

The following day the climber was unable to bear any weight on the injured knee. The guides felt it was unlikely she would improve in the next several days. They concluded that trying to evacuate the climber under their own power would likely lead to further injury, and they made a formal request for NPS assistance with the evacuation from the 14,200-foot camp to the 11,000-foot camp, at which point they felt they could safely continue the evacuation unassisted. Given the forecasted weather, rangers Mike Shain and Joey McBrayer decided an immediate descent was best.

The patient was rigged in a Cascade litter with four NPS staff attending on skis. The team started their descent at 6:40 p.m. The ALP-9 guides were tasked with facilitating their own descent to the 11,000-foot camp with the patient's equipment. The NPS team switched from skis to crampons at the top of Squirrel Hill and continued the lower without incident. Due to the deep snow conditions, a belay rope was never necessary. Both teams arrived at the 11,000-foot camp at 10:30 p.m. The ALP-9 team arrived at

[Below] When moving up or down the fixed lines on Denali's West Buttress, climbers should stay about 10 to 12 meters apart and use the lines only for balance. *NPS Photo*

the 7,200-foot camp the following morning and flew out via their scheduled fixed-wing aircraft. The climber later reported to NPS staff via email that she'd sustained a partial tear of her right anterior cruciate ligament (ACL) and required surgery. [*Source: Denali National Park Supplemental Case Incident Record.*]

ANALYSIS

Each year the Denali rangers and commercial guide services join forces to maintain parallel fixed lines on the headwall above the 14,200-foot camp leading to the crest of the West Buttress. During peak season, large crowds of climbers may develop, moving up and down the fixed lines. Lead Mountaineering Ranger Coley Gentzel has provided the following tips for efficient and safer travel on the fixed lines:

• Use the lines only for balance. Climb the snow and ice.
• Don't trust the lines and anchors implicitly. Keep your eyes up and evaluate everything around you for safety concerns.
• Have a plan for communication—being able to stop, start, and communicate when you are clipping and unclipping the ropes around fixed protection is key to moving efficiently on the lines.
• Climbers in a team should be 10 to 12 meters apart. Too much space between climbers causes difficulties with communication and passing fixed protection.
• A short lanyard is easiest to manage. You should be able to weight the lanyard attached to your ascender while still reaching the ascender easily.
• Make sure everything you're carrying on your body or pack is secure. Dropped items falling down the headwall can be deadly.
• Reorganize your team at the top and bottom of the lines. Keep moving once you are on the lines.

ARIZONA

RAPPEL FAILURE | Inadequate Anchor, Inadequate Belay
CAMELBACK MOUNTAIN

Just after sunrise on August 8, Phoenix firefighter Gary Johnstone, 50, and three teenage boys set up a short rappel (about 40 feet) at an outcrop known as the "Sugar Cube" that is frequently used for rappelling practice. Their anchor was a single, large eyebolt cemented into the rock. One boy, Johnstone's son, successfully rappelled to the ground. The second boy had started his rappel, belayed by Johnstone from the top of the cliff using a strand of the same rope, when the connection to the bolt anchor apparently failed. The rappeller fell to the ground, and both Johnstone and the third boy fell or were pulled off the top as well. Johnstone and one of the boys, Trevor Crouse, 15, later died from their injuries. The other boy who fell survived.

ANALYSIS

Although this was not a climbing accident, it involved misuse or failure of climbing systems and equipment. Johnstone, who had rappelling experience and served with the fire department's technical rescue team, had set up the rappel with an orange sling either tied through the anchor bolt or clipped to it as the primary anchor. As backup, Johnstone was belaying the rappellers with one end of the rappel rope as they descended.

Investigators found the bolt intact. The sling used for the primary anchor has since disappeared, but was seen in a photograph taken by a hiker moments before the accident. This orange sling appeared very similar to another sling found among Johnstone's equipment at the crag, and this second sling had been tied with a flat overhand bend instead of the standard water knot (a.k.a. ring bend.) The flat overhand is known to "roll" under load. Although the flat overhand can be used safely for joining climbing ropes for rappels (leaving tails 10 to 12 inches long in case of rolling), it is not recommended for joining the ends of nylon webbing, which is slipperier than rope. If this method was used to tie the anchor sling that day, it's likely the sling held the weight of the first rappeller but the flat overhand bend rolled and loosened, without being observed, until it reached the point that the knot failed as the second rappeller started down the cliff.

It's unknown why the two people on top of the cliff fell, nor is it clear how Johnstone had anchored himself as he belayed the rappellers. If Johnstone had tied the rappel rope into the anchor sling and the rappellers were descending a single strand, he may have been anchored with the second strand and using the remainder of that strand to belay. His anchor thus would have failed when the sling failed. Or he may have had a separate anchor that also failed. The other boy on top reportedly was tethered to Johnstone and so either was pulled off when the older man fell or was entangled in the rope when the primary anchor failed.

Two key lessons emerge from this unfortunate incident: 1) Tied nylon slings must be joined with a water knot (ring bend) with tails at least two to three inches long protruding from the knot; and 2) Each climber or rappeller at an anchor station should be tethered to the primary anchor or a solid back-up. Although there are times (such as cramped belay transitions) when it makes sense for one climber to anchor temporarily to another, the securest method is to clip or tie into the primary anchor independently. (*Source: The Editors, with information from news reports and correspondence with Phoenix New Times reporter Ray Stern.*)

ROCKFALL

QUEEN CREEK CANYON, UPPER DEVILS CANYON

On February 23, John Scott, 66, died when he was struck in the head by a falling rock while belaying. Scott had just lowered his partner from a sport climb called Projectiles (5.7) at the Lost Wall when a large rock (described as two feet in diameter) fell approximately 55 feet from the top of the cliff and hit Scott at the base of the route. He died at the scene. (*Source: Mountain Project and news reports.*)

ANALYSIS

John Scott was an experienced climber. The rope was running through a bolted anchor at the lip of the cliff, and it is not known what caused the block of volcanic tuff to fall. Scott's partner yelled "Rock!" but Scott was unable to avoid the impact. Given the size of the falling block, a helmet could not prevent serious injury. (*Source: The Editors.*)

CALIFORNIA

ROCKFALL | Poor Position, Inexperience
MT. SHASTA, AVALANCHE GULCH

On the morning of January 1, three climbers (one male and two female, all in their early 20s) were ascending Avalanche Gulch. At 11,500 feet they suffered varying injuries from a natural rockfall event. They called 911 around 9:30 a.m. With head and leg injuries, the climbers requested an urgent rescue. Climbing ranger Nick Meyers called the reporting party's cell phone and spoke with the male climber, who said there were "head and leg injuries and major bleeding...we need help now!" The man's tone was frantic and urgent. Meyers immediately made a plan to launch a helicopter rescue.

Meyers flew to ca 11,000 feet and off-loaded with only his personal gear and medical equipment to climb up to the injured party, where the helicopter would lower the necessary equipment for evacuation. Given the hazardous location, with rockfall and an icy slope, and the critical condition of the injured climbers, the goal was simple: package and transport each patient quickly, then get out of there. At approximately 12:30 p.m. the first critical climber was hoisted from the location and flown to Mercy Redding. The male climber was hoisted soon after and brought to Mercy Mt. Shasta. The third climber was assisted by foot to Lake Helen and was airlifted to Mercy Mt. Shasta. (*Source: Mt. Shasta Wilderness Climbing Ranger Report, prepared by Nick Meyers.*)

ANALYSIS

Mt. Shasta has notoriously loose rock, and this group chose a poor time to climb the peak. Typically in January there can be good snow climbing conditions, but this year the mountain did not receive measurable snow until mid-February. The mountain looked as bare as it might in late summer, and Avalanche Gulch was completely devoid of snow except for a thin strip leading up and to the right of the Heart (the standard route up Avalanche Gulch). A climbing advisory was posted online, at the ranger station, and at the trailhead. Despite all this, the group chose to head out anyway. There was nobody else on the route that day, for good reason.

Climbing directly up the gut of Avalanche Gulch put them in a poor position. Climbers should know that on Shasta any rocks that come off the Red Banks or upper parts of the mountain all funnel into the gut of Avalanche Gulch. As this rescue took place, the party's location was directly in line with all rockfall, and during the rescue the helicopter triggered more rockfall onto the rescuers.

For any mountain with common rockfall, not just Shasta, some things can be done

[Next page] The majority of accidents occur on the south side of Mt. Shasta (shown here), in or near Avalanche Gulch. The hot spot for traumatic accidents is within the oval marked around the Heart. According to Mt. Shasta's accident statistics, the most common climbing accidents involve male climbers, 21–35 years of age, with little to no experience, slipping and falling on snow/ice while descending, with resulting injuries of fractures or sprains. It's extremely common for climbers to get off-route and lost on the upper mountain. If climbing Mt. Shasta, prepare yourself by studying the layout of the mountain, practice snow climbing techniques, and know how to navigate in poor weather. *Google Earth, with assistance from Nick Meyers*

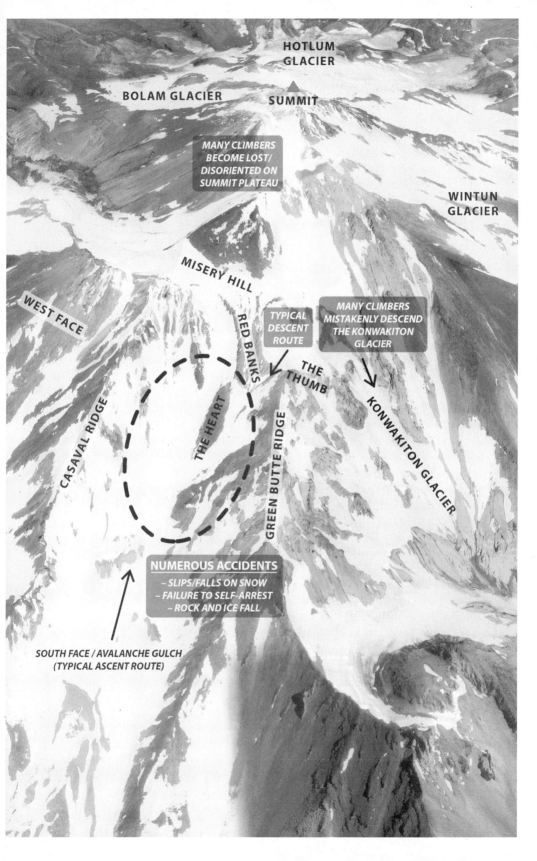

HOTLUM
GLACIER

BOLAM GLACIER

SUMMIT

WINTUN
GLACIER

MANY CLIMBERS
BECOME LOST/
DISORIENTED ON
SUMMIT PLATEAU

MISERY HILL

WEST FACE

RED BANKS

TYPICAL
DESCENT
ROUTE

THE
THUMB

MANY CLIMBERS
MISTAKENLY DESCEND
THE KONWAKITON
GLACIER

THE HEART

CASAVAL RIDGE

GREEN BUTTE RIDGE

KONWAKITON GLACIER

NUMEROUS ACCIDENTS
– SLIPS/FALLS ON SNOW
– FAILURE TO SELF-ARREST
– ROCK AND ICE FALL

SOUTH FACE / AVALANCHE GULCH
(TYPICAL ASCENT ROUTE)

to avoid incident: (1) Don't climb when rock slopes are exposed. (2) Wear a helmet! (3) Limit your time in exposed areas and have a plan should rock or ice come down on you—that is, where is your safety zone should rockfall occur? (4) Climb early in the day, when it's generally colder, rather than later (generally warmer). (5) In a gully or terrain funnel you're asking for trouble. (Avalanche Gulch near the Heart is a perfect example.) Move laterally right and left up the slope to limit time in the "bowling alley." (6) Be extremely careful when walking on low-angle terrain above high-angle terrain— or when moving through any rocky area, for that matter—where a loose rock could be kicked onto climbers below. (*Source: Nick Meyers, Mt. Shasta Climbing Ranger.*)

OFF ROUTE | Party Separated, Weather, Inexperience
MT. SHASTA, RED BANKS / AVALANCHE GULCH

On May 17 a female climber (mid-40s) summited Shasta by the Red Banks/Avalanche Gulch route at roughly 12:15 p.m. She rested on the summit and descended as clouds began to move in, following tracks down the Clear Creek route, where she made contact with another climbing party. This party informed her she was on the Clear Creek route and to head back to the Avalanche Gulch route. The female climber descended further in poor visibility while trying to head skier's right back toward Avalanche Gulch. She placed a call to her climbing party informing them that she was lost (the party had separated due to different climbing paces).

Her climbing party made contact with climbing ranger Brett Wagenheim at roughly 2:30 p.m. to notify him of the situation. Just after 3 p.m., the climber called and informed the ranger that she was lost in a whiteout. Brett concluded that she was likely on the Konwakiton Glacier, above the Mud Creek drainage, but her elevation was unknown. The climber was advised to ascend northwest to the base of Misery Hill; however, she refused to ascend, citing steep terrain, post-holing snow conditions, and poor visibility. Brett advised the climber to call 911 (in order to get coordinates from her cell phone) and to alert Siskiyou Search and Rescue. It was discovered that her location was on the upper mountain (above 12,000 feet) and she was advised to ascend the Konwakiton Glacier. Upon hearing her rough location and descent options, the climber took advantage of a window of improved visibility and was able to ascend west toward the Red Banks and Thumb Rock.

Around 5 p.m. the weather began to deteriorate, with light hail and high winds picking up on the upper mountain. Two wilderness rangers made physical contact with the lost climber at the Red Banks at 6:20 p.m. They assisted her descent to Helen Lake (base of the Avalanche Gulch route), at which point Wagenheim continued to descend with the lost climber to the trailhead, arriving at Bunny Flat at 11:30 p.m. (*Source: Mt. Shasta Wilderness Climbing Ranger Report, prepared by Nick Meyers.*)

ANALYSIS

Group separation can lead to many problems: Is group gear spread among party members? Are all climbers familiar with equipment use, glissading, route-finding, etc.? This issue occurs often among "meet up" groups. These individuals don't know each other's abilities, and as fitness disparities arise there seems to be an attitude of "I'm in this for myself," causing a lack of accountability for fellow party members. (As opposed to the traditional climbing partners' attitude of being with a good friend, and there is no way you're going to adopt the see-ya-back-at-the-trailhead attitude.) In this case, however, this was not a meet-up group.

The lost female climber was the last member of the party to summit. Before summiting, the party agreed to meet back at Lake Helen, where they had camped. It should be noted that the party left this climber alone on the upper mountain, out of water, unfamiliar with the route or descent, in poor visibility, and late in the day.

All routes on Shasta first surmount the summit plateau that lies between 12,800 and 13,500 feet; then one must proceed to the summit pinnacle. During the descent across the summit plateau in low-visibility situations, it is common for people to become disoriented and unable to determine which way to descend. This results in extensive, time-consuming searches and exposes lost climbers to big-mountain hazards. The Shasta climbing rangers do their best to inform people of route-finding issues and have even resorted to "wanding" the route at times (though wands carry their own problems, as they fall down or create a false sense of security).

Any climber on Shasta should study the terrain before climbing and be skilled in basic navigation and route-finding. It's very easy to wander off the wrong side into heavily glaciated terrain. In this scenario, do you carry the necessary equipment for a high-elevation open bivouac in a storm? Group separation is not recommended, and in this case made the climber's descent complicated and potentially dangerous. (*Source: Nick Meyers, Mt. Shasta Climbing Ranger.*)

SLIP ON SNOW | Failure to Self-Arrest, No Helmet
MT. SHASTA, AVALANCHE GULCH / HEART ROUTE

On May 25 a female climber (58) was ascending Avalanche Gulch via the Heart at roughly 12,000 feet, just below the Red Banks, when she fell and lost control of her ice axe. She was then unable to arrest her fall and was stopped/tackled by an independent climber after sliding to 11,400 feet, at climber's right of the Heart, near a well-trodden boot pack. A bystander called 911 at roughly 8:30 a.m., and the climbing rangers were dispatched thereafter.

Climbing rangers Nick Meyers and Brett Wagenheim were on the route and arrived on scene by 8:45 a.m. The climber complained of left ankle pain, had small lacerations and abrasions to her face and arms, and was not wearing a helmet. The climber was noticeably shivering and breathing rapidly. She was covered in an emergency bivouac for warmth, which helped reduce her breathing/ventilation rate. Icefall and rockfall continued to be a concern. The climber was able to bear weight on her left ankle and was assisted by short-rope on the descent to Helen Lake. The climber received further treatment of her abrasions at Helen Lake. She declined further assistance from rangers and self-rescued from Helen down to Bunny Flat with the assistance of her climbing party. (*Source: Mt. Shasta Wilderness Climbing Ranger Report, prepared by Nick Meyers.*)

ANALYSIS

Climbers should familiarize themselves with the proper techniques for ascending easy to moderate snow and ice, especially when climbing unroped. Practicing self-arrest techniques *before* a climb will lead to greater success in arresting a fall. "Know the Ropes" in *Accidents 2014* covered essential snow climbing techniques. Search *publications.americanalpineclub.org* to find this helpful article. (*Source: The Editors.*)

ROCKFALL | Poor Position

MT. SHASTA, WINTUN ROUTE

On July 29 a male climber (58) was descending the Wintun Route when he was hit by rockfall at 11,700 feet. The climber fractured his femur and arm. There was also bruising to his hip. Nick Meyers was notified at about 4:30 p.m. A California Highway Patrol helicopter was requested for evacuation, which was accomplished by hoisting the injured climber using a screamer suit. The hoist occurred at about 5:30 p.m. Rangers aided the rescue over the phone only. (*Source: Mt. Shasta Wilderness Climbing Ranger Report, prepared by Nick Meyers.*)

ANALYSIS

This climber was quite unlucky. The Wintun Route is relatively mellow and has not had many accidents over the years. Since it's not very steep, rockfall is uncommon. The group was led by experienced guides. It's likely that a single, basketball-size rock released from nearly 1,000 feet above and impacted the climber, breaking his leg and arm. The group could have stuck closer to the ridgeline. This would not have made travel much more difficult and likely would have prevented this accident. Being off the ridgeline, they were more exposed to falling objects. But, again, this was a very unlucky incident. (*Source: Nick Meyers, Mt. Shasta Climbing Ranger.*)

FALL ON ROCK | Exceeding Abilities, Off-Route

TUOLUMNE MEADOWS, LEMBERT DOME, NORTHWEST BOOKS

It's 10 a.m. on August 13 on Lembert Dome. Clank, clank, clunk. A yellow object shoots down the cliff. Jeff Los and I (both 23) start to chuckle at the thought of Curtis Burrowes (24) having to buy another number 2 Camalot. But laughter soon turns to concern as the rope pulls taut on my right hand and a scream pierces through spiraling gusts of wind. Curtis had disappeared around the corner nearly 20 minutes earlier with the intention of leading the second pitch (5.6) of Northwest Books. From our vantage, we couldn't see his actual fall—just the yellow cam shooting across the sky—but a few hikers below call up to tell us that Curtis isn't looking good.

Soon, a faint voice murmurs, "I'm okay." I decide to tie in while Jeff belays me up to Curtis' position. Serendipitously, an EMT is below, and he quickly free solos up to Curtis' perch to help. Curtis is in rough shape: a possible concussion, severe back pain, disoriented, and he can't move. Instead of climbing the 5.6 pitch, he had opted to climb a 5.9 variation—a daunting task for a new trad climber. He fell 40 feet and hit some ledges on the way down. He had fallen while trying to place the yellow cam. After a call to YOSAR, rescuers arrived with a litter in tow. Curtis was lowered down the cliff by litter, and Jeff and I, along with YOSAR, wheeled Curtis down to the parking lot. From there he was transferred by ambulance to Mammoth Lakes Hospital.

ANALYSIS

Curtis made it out relatively unscathed, with abrasions, a bruised back, and broken tailbone. He had only five to six months of trad climbing experience before this climb, and only up to 5.7. While getting off-route posed a problem, he made a further mistake by running it out because he was too pumped to set protection (even though many options were available). In this instance he should have downclimbed instead of running it out. Jeff and I could not see Curtis well, as he was around the corner, so we will never know how much slack was out. (*Source: Justin Raphaelson.*)

FALL ON ROCK | Off-Route

TUOLUMNE MEADOWS, FAIRVIEW DOME, REGULAR ROUTE

On June 21, 2013, I (61 years old, experienced climber) set out to climb the Regular Route (III 5.9) up the north face of Fairview Dome. I had climbed the route at least a few times before, including rope-soloing the climb. Thus, while leading the fourth pitch, well beyond the crux moves, I was quite surprised to fall.

My flight and slide seemed pretty long (20–30 feet), though my belayer (56 years old) was able to reel in some rope before it softly caught me. Steep terrain allowed for a pretty clean fall, but I managed to fully rupture my left Achilles tendon. Once my partner lowered me to the belay ledge, I found that I had no strength or control in my foot, and that the normally thick, cord-like tendon resembled mushy, soft tissue.

Generously, a party of two climbing below offered to rappel with us, allowing for two-rope rappels. At the base of the route, I was able to scramble down to the trail and hike out to my vehicle using my left heel. While my partner broke down our camp, I visited with the Tuolumne SAR team to see if they could confirm my self-diagnosis of a ruptured Achilles tendon. We reached the hospital a few hours later. I had the separated Achilles tendon surgically reattached a week later. I resumed climbing after six months of recovery.

ANALYSIS

While I had done the route before, it's possible that I got off route. Even with the crux climbing behind me, the potential consequences of falling were not over. I could have paid closer attention to the terrain. (*Source: Anonymous.*)

FALL ON ROCK | Free Soloing, Off-Route

TUOLUMNE MEADOWS, MATTHES CREST

Late in the afternoon on August 16, Bradley Parker (36) was free soloing the Matthes Crest ridge traverse (III 5.7) when he fell approximately 300 feet to his death. Several climbers witnessed his fall. Earlier in the day, Parker and his girlfriend, Jainee Dial, had climbed the Southeast Buttress of Cathedral Peak (II 5.6) as a roped team. When they returned to the base at 4 p.m., Parker went on to attempt the Matthes Crest alone. (This is a standard linkup for fit alpine climbers.) Meanwhile, Dial hiked back to the trailhead; their plan was to meet at the trailhead between 6:30 and 7:30 p.m.

Parker passed two parties in the notch between the north and south summits prior to his fall. The first group stated later that Parker complained to them of dehydration and leg cramps; however, they noticed nothing in his movement or behavior that indicated distress. Parker then passed Brian Martin (YOSAR member) and his partner. Both Martin and his partner described Parker as climbing competently, quickly, and fluidly as he followed the most popular route toward the north summit.

About 15 minutes after Parker passed them, at approximately 5:45 p.m., both parties in the notch and two other teams at the base all heard a combination of yelling and something falling. They saw an unroped climber fall from the top of the ridge near the north summit. A climber at the base, an off-duty paramedic, ran up the hill to where Parker had stopped, but he was obviously deceased. NPS personnel recovered Parker's body via helicopter short-haul the following morning.

ANALYSIS

Bradley Parker was an expert climber with around 15 years of experience. He regularly free soloed easy routes in the Sierra. According to Dial, Parker was in excellent physical condition. When she initially reported him missing at 9 p.m., she was very concerned because he usually was so dependable. On August 16 the weather at Matthes was sunny, clear, and calm. Although the climbers Parker passed said they heard him complain of cramps, dehydration, and possible blisters on his toes, there is no way to know if these ailments had anything to do with Parker's fall. None of the witnesses saw the start of his fall and none noticed any rockfall.

On August 19, I (Jesse McGahey) went to the scene with Brian Martin to investigate the accident. From the ground, Martin described and pointed out the location of the start of Parker's fall. Martin and I then climbed to the north summit. At the register we found that Parker had signed a 3" x 5" note card, which read "BP OG, beautiful sunset... Cathedral Matthes link up, w/Jainee (Mid-Aug 2014)."

We then climbed down to the approximate location from which he had fallen, a distinct "V notch" north of the north summit. Directly above the notch is a 5.8 downclimb of parallel cracks with good rock. If Parker had fallen while downclimbing he would have fallen to the east side of the Matthes ridge and not to the west—where he ended up. From the V notch most climbers then head north on the east side of the ridge on small ledge systems. For Parker to fall to the west, he would have had to traverse a 10-foot-wide fin of steep, seldom-traveled rock on the west face of the ridge. Though we saw one potential rock scar about six inches long, where a hold could have broken, there is no way to know if the hold broke when Parker grabbed it.

According to Dial, Parker had soloed Matthes Crest several times, possibly even a couple of weeks before his fall. However, one of the witnesses recalled asking Parker as he passed her party, "Which way does the route go from here [to the north summit?]" and that he had seemed unsure, saying something to the effect of, "I think it goes up this way." Parker was free soloing. Regardless of what occurred at the moment he lost control, without protection or helmet the 300-foot fall was unsurvivable. (*Source: Jesse McGahey, Yosemite National Park Ranger.*)

OFF ROUTE | Weather, Darkness, Party Separated
MT. CONNESS, NORTH RIDGE

On July 17, brothers Bruce Porter (58) and Bob Porter (61) attempted the north ridge (III 5.7) of Mt. Conness (12,600'). After a thunderstorm forced a retreat, they chose a longer, more difficult route back to the trailhead, resulting in a bivy at 11,000 feet without gear. The next morning they separated, attempting different routes back to Conness Lakes. They were reported missing that morning and found by NPS rescuers that afternoon. (*Source: Jesse McGahey, Yosemite National Park Ranger.*)

ANALYSIS

I am 61 years old and lack the fitness, stamina and strength I once possessed. Good judgment is everything in the mountains. Sadly, good judgment is often gained by using poor judgment and learning from it. We should have retreated down the route instead of an unknown descent. Our worst decision was separating without a clear plan. (*Source: Bob Porter.*)

Bruce and Bob knew the predicted weather and had experienced thunderstorms for two days before their climb. Like many climbers facing inclement weather, they decided the summit attempt was worth the risk. Although the storm spared Conness, they made the correct decision to retreat, given the threat. To their credit, Bob and Bruce had a map, layers, a fire kit, and headlamps, all of which came in handy. (*Source: Jesse McGahey, Yosemite National Park Ranger.*)

FALL ON ROCK | Protection Pulled Out

EL CAPITAN, NORTH AMERICA WALL

On the last day of my junior year of high school, I packed up the car and headed for Yosemite Valley. I hoped to make it up El Capitan as many times as possible over the summer. The previous summer I had learned how to aid and big-wall climb and made four ascents of El Cap. This summer would not go as planned.

My partner Ken and I immediately decided on a five-day push up the North America Wall, starting June 6. I was going to lead the first pitch. After 20 feet of easy climbing, I went into aid mode, placing two small cams. The next placement was the one that ruined my summer. Standing on the cam, looking for my next placement, I noticed a cool spot to hand-place a beak (just below another perfect small cam placement). After a few short seconds...PING!! The beak popped and I fell 12 feet onto the lower cam. It was a short fall and relatively clean, but it was clear I had broken my ankle. Ken lowered me to the ground, and we went from being a couple of stoked monkeys to a couple of very, very sad monkeys.

Ken, an EMT, quickly made a splint with climbing tape, a spork, and a nut tool. Before descending, we recruited a friend to help carry down my gear. It took a long time to crawl down the talus past the base of Mescalito, the base of the Nose, and finally to the El Cap Meadow bridge. An X-ray revealed a fracture, and I was out for the next 10 weeks.

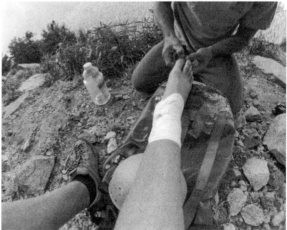

ANALYSIS

The lesson I learned from this was simple: Don't place crappy gear for fun. Thankfully, I've recovered and climbed El Cap twice since the incident. (*Source: Mickey Sensenbach.*)

[Above] The result of placing poor protection: a broken ankle and an impromptu splint from tape, a nut tool, and a spork. *Mickey Sensenbach*

FALL ON ROCK | Misjudged Pendulum
EL CAPITAN, THE NOSE

On May 30 a climber took a large pendulum fall while attempting the King Swing (a 100-foot pendulum from Boot Flake to Eagle Ledge) on the Nose route (VI 5.9 C2) of El Capitan. During the pendulum, the climber failed to gain holds allowing him to climb toward Eagle Ledge and consequently fell uncontrollably back across the wall, colliding with Boot Flake. Another climber on the wall witnessed the fall and called 911 to alert rescuers. The witness said the injured climber had taken a 100-foot, arcing pendulum fall, and afterward he had hung at the end of his rope unconscious for several minutes. After the accident he regained consciousness but complained of significant neck and chest pain, and had a large bruise on the back of his head. The climber's partners eventually lowered him to a stance behind Texas Flake.

Because of the potentially significant injuries and decreasing daylight, two park medics were short-hauled to the patient. After an assessment, the medics determined it was safe to spend the night out and that they would lower the patient to the ground in the morning. The rangers monitored the patient as the three individuals spent the night on top of El Cap Tower. At first light the patient was lowered to the ground by a rescue team on the summit and sent to a nearby medical facility.

ANALYSIS

The climber was experienced and had reportedly climbed El Cap twice before—once via the Nose and once via the Salathé Wall, 20 years prior. Most climbers are lowered to several meters below Boot Flake before attempting the King Swing. However, the climber was not lowered sufficiently. According to the witness, the climber reportedly hit Boot Flake during his return swing, after losing control above Eagle Ledge.

Many people underestimate the speed and force that can be generated by a pendulum fall and the danger of striking an obstacle during a swing. These falls can potentially generate the same force as a vertical fall and can leave major organs and the head and spine more vulnerable to impact. While performing a pendulum, it is important to be aware of your surroundings and to assess obstacles that could be encountered while swinging across a wall in either direction. Head impact is the most serious injury you may encounter while climbing—always wear a helmet. (*Source: Cameron King, Yosemite National Park Ranger.*)

STRANDED | Inexperience, Darkness, Weather
HALF DOME, SNAKE DIKE

On March 8, Ryan Ellis (23), Kristen Elford (27), Charles Celerier (22), and Ken Langley (26) set out to climb the Snake Dike route (8 pitches, 5.7) on Half Dome, intending to take the cable descent from the summit. The climbers were new to multi-pitch climbing, and this was Kristen's first climb outdoors. The team researched the route and asked friends for advice, and the weather was fair with warm days and cold nights. They started their hike from the Valley around 7 a.m., but got off-route on the approach, which cost them a little time. While hiking they did not see any snow or signs that there would be snow on the top of Half Dome.

Once at the start of the climb, the team decided to climb as a group of four, with one leader and the other three following each pitch. The climb went without serious incident; they were just slower than anticipated. The group was still on the climb as the sun set, and they got to the top in the dark. There they realized the summit area was covered in snow and ice, and they were unable to locate the cables, which were buried. They were stranded.

At approximately 9:30 p.m., Ryan called 911 to ask for a rescue. The park dispatcher informed them that rescue was not possible until morning. Keeping in touch with dispatch throughout the night, the group huddled and survived a cold, brutal night on the summit with minimal food and water and only two of them having warm clothes. The next morning two rangers climbed Snake Dike, starting their approach at around 5 a.m., and reached the stranded party around 10 a.m. The rescuers assisted the climbers in rappelling the route and hiking out to their vehicles.

ANALYSIS

Charles did not remember checking weather for that week, but remembers the weather being nice. He also remembers getting advice from a friend who told him that the cables could be difficult to find, especially if they were covered in snow. (Snake Dike climbs the sunny southwest face of Half Dome, while the cables are on the much colder east face.) Kristen and Charles both reported that an earlier start could have helped their group succeed, and that climbing as a team of four presented problems of rope management, which slowed them down.

This is a good reminder to check with other climbers, climbing forums or online trip reports, and rangers for updated conditions on climbs. In the end, the climbers rappelled the route with rescuers, demonstrating that this was a possible way out of their predicament. Always be prepared to reverse a route if the descent is inaccessible or you can't locate it. Short days, limited knowledge of the seasonal conditions, and a lack of climbing experience resulted in a long, arduous day of route-finding and rope management, ending in being stranded in dangerously low temperatures. (*Source: Kristin Anderson, Yosemite National Park Ranger.*)

AVALANCHE | Climbing Unroped, Weather, Poor Position
LAUREL MOUNTAIN, EAST FACE, MENDENHALL COULOIR

On April 6 my partner (age 44) and I (age 29) set out to climb Laurel Mountain (11,812') via the Mendenhall Couloir (3,000', III, Class 4, Steep Snow). We started hiking around 8 a.m. and reached the base of the couloir by 8:45 a.m. The weather was clear and the air temperature around 40°F. The couloir contained enough snow for a winter-style ascent, but there was not enough snow to descend on skis, with exposed rocks and bare spots. We dug a snow pit right at the base to check the snow conditions, and there was no indication of a weak layer. Everything seemed consolidated. But it was warm, especially as we went up.

We carried winter gear, crampons, ice tools, avalanche beacons, helmets, a rope, and some rock protection. This was our first time in the couloir, and we wanted to be prepared in case we needed to set belays. However, we were climbing unroped, as we felt the conditions were quite within our moderate level of experience (the snow was 45° or less). We initially climbed with crampons until reaching a 30-foot rock slab. The remaining ascent was without crampons.

By 10 a.m. we'd gained 1,500 feet and were halfway up the mountain. At this point there is a band of red-colored rock and the gully splits. I heard a low rumble and looked up to see a snow cloud coming down the right-side gully. We immediately took a few steps to the left. Just to the right of my partner, a step away from clearing the slide, I was caught and carried downward. I tried to self-arrest, but there was too much snow sliding beneath me. I lost grip of my ice axe and struggled to stay atop. Throughout my slide, I fought to grab onto rocks and reorient myself. I fell over a few large drops, including the 30-foot rock slab. Near the bottom, after sliding and falling around 1,000 feet, I was able to hold onto a ledge and stop.

Luckily I was not buried and was able to extricate myself from the snow. I found a small ledge where I could drop my backpack, patted myself down for injuries, and yelled, "I'm okay!" Within seconds I heard my partner calling for me. After making visual and audible contact, I asked that he move away from the gully and onto the rock. It took him 15 minutes or so to downclimb to me. My right thumb was bleeding; I also felt pain in my left hip, tailbone, and right knee. While waiting for my partner, my hands and fingers started to tingle and shake. I felt exhausted and just wanted to sleep. After my partner reached me, I took 600mg of ibuprofen and we were able to walk out to Convict Lake without further incident.

A doctor's visit revealed abrasions to my hands and hip and increased curvature in my tailbone, possibly due to a high-impact fall. I also continued to have tingling and shaking for 10-plus hours.

ANALYSIS

This was a wet-snow avalanche with small to medium-size snowballs; it contained no fresh snow and was very heavy and clumpy. The Eastern Sierra Avalanche Center advisory for the day had mentioned low to moderate risk for east-facing slopes, like the one we were on. The warm weather was likely the main factor in this slide. It's also likely that our position on the open, upper slope was too centered; we should have climbed along the side of the couloir. However, lower sections of the couloir are so chute-like it would be impossible to climb out of the avalanche path. [*Source: Anonymous.*]

[*Editor's note: With an earlier start these climbers likely could have climbed the couloir before the snow heated up dangerously. Ascents of east-facing snow climbs in the spring and summer are best started before dawn.*]

LIGHTNING | Exposure, Weather, Poor Position
BEAR CREEK SPIRE, NORTH ARÊTE

On August 9 my partner Matt and I (both 26) attempted to climb Bear Creek Spire via the North Arête (6 pitches, 5.8) in a single-day, car-to-car push from the trailhead at Mosquito Flats. The weather report called for a 20 percent chance of scattered thunderstorms after 11 a.m. We started up the route at around 9 a.m. At this time we had bluebird skies and good temps. We made it to within about 200 feet of the summit by noon, when the weather quickly took a turn for the worse. Clouds began rolling in from the west, and it soon began snowing and hailing, with rolls of thunder in the distance. Our situation was difficult: We were between the North Arête and Northeast Ridge routes, on fourth- and fifth-class terrain and fairly close to the summit ridge. I

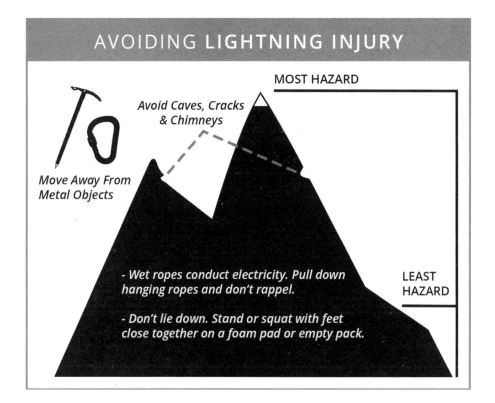

AVOIDING LIGHTNING INJURY

MOST HAZARD

Avoid Caves, Cracks & Chimneys

Move Away From Metal Objects

- Wet ropes conduct electricity. Pull down hanging ropes and don't rappel.

- Don't lie down. Stand or squat with feet close together on a foam pad or empty pack.

LEAST HAZARD

was aware of only two descent options. The first and most ideal was a rappel from the summit blocks, which we ruled out due to the danger of continuing upward; second was a descent by the Northeast Ridge. We resolved to downclimb and rappel the latter as quickly as possible.

Shortening the rope, we began simul-climbing in worsening conditions across the face between the North Arête and Northeast Ridge, and then down the ridge itself. Several things then happened in rapid succession, and the sequence is difficult to piece together. On the ridge, Matt told me he could hear the rock humming, and we became increasingly frightened. We unroped. I saw flashes of light on some nearby rocks. I was looking at Matt and saw what looked like a very small explosion (like a firecracker) on or near his helmet. I could smell smoke, sort of like gunpowder. He said, "I think something just happened to me." We continued downclimbing, unroped, on snow- and hail-covered rock.

After descending 100 feet, we experienced thunder and lightning in increasing intervals. Soon there was no lapse between flash and sound. We were panicked and felt extremely exposed. At some point in our downclimbing, we found a small cave. We both crawled into it. I asked Matt if he had been struck by lightning, to which he responded that he had. He described feeling a "buzzing" feeling in his head and that he could smell burning in his nose. He then showed me a small burn on his thumb, where the charge appeared to have left his body. He otherwise displayed no symptoms.

As we waited in the cave, I began to experience the first symptoms of hypothermia. I had trouble accomplishing simple tasks, like coiling the rope or stowing my climbing rack. We were soaked and the temperature had dropped dramatically. The lightning began to ease, and even though it was hailing heavily we made the decision to continue down. After five to ten minutes without lightning or thunder we made a break for it. We downclimbed the ridgeline for another 100 feet and then rappelled to the steep talus field below. From here, we were able to climb off the Northeast Ridge.

I have WFR certification, and I made some basic assessments of Matt's condition on the ground, mostly concerned about any changes in level of responsiveness and behavior. This was done rapidly and mostly on the fly. He displayed no symptoms other than singed nose hair and pain in the burned finger. With clothes on and calories in, we warmed up quickly as we hiked, and we made it back to the car in good health.

ANALYSIS

We should have sought cover when the clouds first appeared. Although the storm developed rapidly, we might have been able to find some immediate shelter. Our second mistake was trying to descend exposed ridgeline in the heat of the storm. However, we both felt extremely exposed on the upper part of the mountain and in danger of severe hypothermia should we just try to "wait it out." Matt is projected to have permanent hearing loss in one ear. (*Source: Nick Thurston.*)

[*Editor's note: These climbers made tough choices in a serious situation. Descending as soon as the storm approached was a good decision, since the risk of lightning generally is highest near summits. Despite their concerns about hypothermia, taking shelter in the cave was risky. Lightning will jump the gap from the ceiling to the ground below, using a human body as the conductor. The climbers got away with it this time, and the cave might have helped stave off hypothermia, but they were lucky.*

When caught by lightning, climbers should attempt to get off high points and ridgelines, and pull the rope if it's hanging overhead, because a wet rope will conduct current (do not rappel in a lightning storm). Keep away from metal gear such as ice axes, and stay out of cracks or caves. Stand or squat on a foam pad, empty pack, or rope. Minimize contact with the ground—keep your feet together and do not lie down. If forced to shelter in a cave, stand or squat inside, away from the entrance, keeping as much distance between your head and the ceiling as you can without sitting or lying down.]

FALL ON ROCK | Climbing Unroped
PALISADES, TEMPLE CRAG

On August 6 the Inyo County Sheriff's Office was contacted by a hiker who reported an abandoned campsite near Third Lake. Deputies learned the camp belonged to Brenton Wright (27), who had been in the Sierra for one month, solo climbing various classic mountain routes. On July 30 he entered the Palisades region with the intention of linking the Temple-Gayley-Sill traverse with the Sill-Thunderbolt traverse. He never returned.

The Inyo County Search and Rescue Team was called upon to locate Wright in this massive area of technical terrain. From the air, Wright's body was located approximately 900 feet above the base of Temple Crag, between the Venusian Blind and Moon Goddess Arête routes. Five SAR members with technical climbing gear were inserted at Third Lake and hiked to his position. The team determined that Wright had fallen nearly 500 feet and sustained fatal injuries. His body was recovered by long line. [*Source: Inyo County Search and Rescue/Victor Lawson.*)

ANALYSIS

Soloing big mountain terrain has potential for big consequences, and any slip can turn fatal. Soloists should be particularly attentive to route-finding, selecting good holds, and minding mountain weather. (*Source: The Editors.*)

LOWERING ERROR | Poor Position
MICKEY'S BEACH, THE EGG

It was a beautiful Saturday in July for top-roping climbs at Mickey's Beach with my buddy Tracy. While belaying him on the Egg formation, I got a great view of him climbing above the ocean and decided to take a photo. Still belaying, I slowly backed up a five-foot-tall ramp of rock, until I was approximately 15 feet from the wall, to frame the shot. I'm a big guy, and although he took a few hangs while climbing they didn't affect me in this stance. Despite my distance from the wall, it didn't feel dangerous, as the belay rope ran nearly vertically up this tall route.

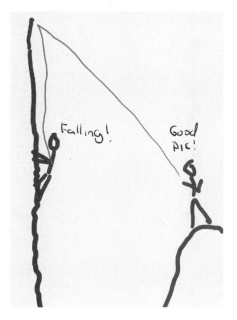

When Tracy completed the route, I began to lower him and I asked him to re-clip a directional I had set up on the route. He grabbed the quickdraw, pulled himself up a bit to clip the rope, and then flopped back. This provided just enough force to lift me off the ramp and swing me into the wall. I was very surprised at the amount of rope stretch, which added velocity to my swing. I hit the wall with my feet extended and my knees locked. All of my weight went into my left foot, and I felt the crunch of bone and the sparkle of

[Above] In this accident, the belayer stepped back to snap a photo of his partner on the wall. When the climber unexpectedly fell, the belayer was pulled hard into the rock and broke his ankle. *Brian Degenhardt*

nerve. Fractured talus. After my swing I continued to lower Tracy to the ground. We pulled our rope, left our gear on the route, and I crawled back up the approach trail.

ANALYSIS

There's plenty of danger to be found in climbing if you're careless. I should have considered my position while belaying as carefully as I do when I'm climbing. (*Source: Brian Degenhardt.*)

FALL ON ROCK | Placed Inadequate Protection
TAHQUITZ ROCK, WEST FACE, THE TROUGH

On July 13, I visited Tahquitz Rock with partner Brian (31) after a few-year hiatus from climbing. I decided to get us started by heading up the Trough (4 pitches, 5.4), a climb well within my ability level. On the first pitch I placed gear every 10 to 15 feet or so and climbed steadily past the first recommended belay ledge. Continuing up the second pitch, I climbed past a fixed piton and placed a small nut above. After this I stopped placing gear. Wanting to ensure I had adequate gear for a solid anchor, and knowing that the climbing was relatively easy, I ran it out.

At a bulge I lost my footing and began pinwheeling down the heavily featured climb, banging against the rock until I landed on a sloping ledge about 60 feet below my high point. My nut held and there was no gear failure. I was able to speak, did not lose consciousness, and my partner was able to call out for help. Meanwhile, I used my remaining gear to make an anchor, and my partner took me off belay. Fortunately, Tony Grice, a local climbing guide, was nearby and facilitated an assisted rappel off the sloping ledge, using the anchor I'd built.

I had my cell phone and we called for an evacuation. Cal Fire facilitated the rescue with the help of Tony and other local climbers. After a high-angle litter carry, I was airlifted to the Riverside Community Medical Center. I was released the following day with minor injuries: a fractured ankle, a sprain, contusions, and hematomas.

ANALYSIS

This is an accident that never should have happened. The mistake is clear and the outcome irrefutably unnecessary. Regardless of how easy a climb is, knowing that a rescue from a cliff requires tremendous effort, expense, and risk should be reason enough to place gear more often. I was cocky, foolhardy, and complacent, and my poor decision-making led to a tremendous effort to extract me from the situation. Even for experienced climbers, a simple "clip" can make all the difference. (*Source: Shannon McMullen, 43.*)

SLIP ON ROCK, RAPPEL ERROR | Alcohol, Poor Position

SAN BERNADINO MOUNTAINS, LUCERNE VALLEY

The following accident occurred on April 9 while climbing at an undeveloped area on Grapevine Road in the Lucerne Valley. Person 1 (37 years old, 25 years of climbing experience) had intentions of establishing a new route on one of the Joshua Tree–like cliffs; he had also been drinking heavily throughout the day. After reaching the top of the cliff, Person 1 tied off a rope to inspect a new climb. Unfortunately, Person 1 connected his rope to a previously established anchor that was designed for highlining (high-level slacklining) rather than climbing. Person 2 had previously warned Person 1 about using these anchors, because they were not designed for a rappel or in a good position to inspect the climb. Person 2 suggested Person 1 place new anchor bolts atop the cliff for better access to the new route; however, Person 1 did not heed this warning.

While standing near the cliff's edge, Person 1 began attaching his Grigri to the rope. Then he suddenly lost his footing (due to drunkenness), causing him to fall backward. Person 1 grabbed the rope with his hands, bounced once against the rock after falling 35 feet, and then swung sideways due to the poor anchor position. After this swing he lost hold of the rope, hitting the ground flat on his back, having fallen a total of 55 to 60 feet. After the impact Person 1 was winded and confused but still conscious and capable of moving all limbs; he could not stand or walk under his own power. Person 2 immediately called Global Rescue and was referred to local dispatch for evacuation of Person 1.

Within 15 minutes of the accident, Person 1 complained of feeling cold and pain in his neck, and Person 2 kept pressure on his neck and covered him with a blanket. A helicopter arrived within 45 minutes of the initial call and evacuated Person 1 to the nearest hospital. Person 2 stayed to inspect gear and clean up the location before joining his partner at the hospital. Person 1 experienced a concussion, a broken neck between C4 and C7, a broken right shoulder blade, and severed nerves in his arms from grabbing the rope during his fall. (*Source: "Person 2," 28 years old, 19 years of climbing experience.*)

ANALYSIS

This accident speaks for itself. Drinking while climbing or working with ropes at heights is not recommended. Additionally, one should only rappel from anchors that are well-positioned and designed with climbing in mind. (*Source: The Editors.*)

FALL ON ROCK | Exceeding Abilities, No Helmet

JOSHUA TREE NATIONAL PARK, HEMINGWAY BUTTRESS, WHITE LIGHTNING

On January 1, Kennya Pimentel (20) of Las Vegas, Nevada, fell while climbing White Lightning (5.7) at the Hemingway Buttress. Unable to place protection or climb through a crux section, she decided to downclimb and lower off from about 100 feet up the climb. However, while downclimbing she fell, swinging and then hitting her hip on the rock and flipping backward. The fall distance was about six feet. She was not wearing a helmet and initially complained of both head and hip injuries. Another climber ascended to her position and suspected possible spinal cord injury. She was stabilized into a seated position but unable to be lowered.

Climbers at the crag notified the Joshua Tree National Park staff, who called for a rescue due to the nature of her injuries. Rangers, volunteers from the JOSAR team, sheriff's officers, and helicopters responded. JOSAR team members helped Pimentel's climbing partner escape the belay and then used a high-angle rescue system to extract Pimentel and safely lower her to the ground. All precautions were taken to stabilize her during the evacuation. She was airlifted to Desert Regional Hospital. Fortunately, upon examination, it was determined she had sustained no serious injury. The rescue took about five hours to complete. (*Sources: Jennie Kish Albrinck, Joshua Tree National Park staff, and David Doucette.*)

ANALYSIS

Climbers should always consider wearing a helmet, even when single-pitch climbing, due to the possibility of dropped objects and swinging falls, flipping upside-down, or impacting ledges and other terrain features. Much of the terrain in Joshua Tree is less than vertical, which increases the potential for head injuries in falls like this.

Additionally, the victim's partner did not know how to escape the belay. They were lucky to be in an area with other climbers who could provide assistance and call for help. Had they been on their own, the rescue could have been delayed significantly due to their lack of mobility. (*Source: The Editors.*)

COLORADO

AVALANCHE | Poor Position
ROCKY MOUNTAIN NATIONAL PARK, LOCH VALE

Loch Vale is a popular north-facing ice climbing area at about 10,000 feet in elevation. At approximately 3 p.m. on December 21, two climbers began to free solo Mo' Flo' Than Go, a short WI2/3 route. They told a group of four climbers who were gathered under the ice curtain on the far left side of the route that they planned to establish a top-rope above a mixed climb farther to the right.

"Within a few minutes," one of the climbers in the second group reported, "we heard a rumble and saw a large amount of snow slide over the ice cliff and run downhill to climber's right from our position. We could not see the other climbers. One of our group called to them to see if they were OK. Climber B had been swept off the top of the flow to the bottom, but he indicated he was OK. Climber A managed to stay on the ice face. One of our climbing ropes had been swept downhill about 20 feet, but otherwise our group was unaffected. We began to pack up and belayed one of our climbers up to recover our top-rope. Climber A downclimbed, took the coiled rope that Climber B had been carrying, and then climbed back up the same route to establish a top-rope.

ANALYSIS
The avalanche appeared to empty much of the steep, north-facing bowl above Mo' Flo' Than Go. Approximately eight inches of new snow had fallen during the day, mostly heavier, wet flakes and some graupel. The snow appears to have slid on top of older, somewhat consolidated snow. This particular climb has a small bowl directly above it

[Below] Diagram of the slide that pulled a climber off Mo' Flo' Than Go in Loch Vale. *Ryan Teter*

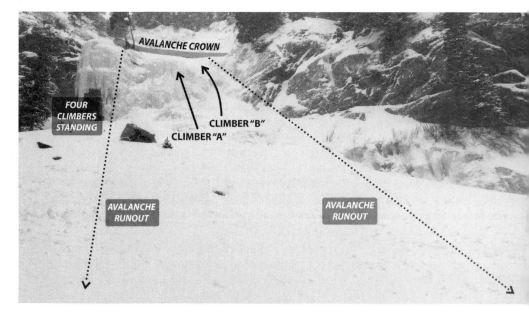

that quickly gets loaded with snow. The person in our party who established our top-rope said he painstakingly avoided the bowl because of the snow deposition. (*Sources: Ryan Teter and Colorado Avalanche Information Center.*)

(*Editor's note: Since ice climbers often are not equipped with avalanche transceivers, shovels, or probes, awareness and prudence are their primary defenses in avalanche terrain. Learn to recognize avalanche-prone terrain and conditions, and read your area's avalanche forecast before climbing in any zone where avalanches are possible.*)

FALL ON ROCK | Inadequate Belay
ROOSEVELT NATIONAL FOREST, DREAM CANYON

On a lovely spring day in April, I met several friends at the Oceanic Wall in Dream Canyon, a deep tributary of Boulder Canyon. After several warm-ups, I got on a 5.11d I had climbed several times in the past. The crux lies between the third and fifth bolts, where the route steepens in a small bulge and the holds are small and far apart. After clipping the third bolt—approximately 30 feet off the ground—I climbed a technical slab adjacent to a small (approximately two to three feet wide), right-facing dihedral with a seam in the corner. Getting to the fourth bolt entails moving over this dihedral to the left, but at this point I couldn't reach the bolt. The third bolt was now about 10 feet below me and slightly to the right, below the dihedral. I started downclimbing to reposition and realized I couldn't reverse the move over the corner. I decided to jump out to clear the dihedral and shouted to my belayer that I was coming off.

I expected to drop well below the dihedral, but instead, as the rope came tight, I swung hard into the wall below the corner and just below the third bolt. I was still in a push-off position so my right knee slammed into the wall, shattering my patella (kneecap). I was lowered to the ground, a distance of about 20 feet.

One of our party had a set of hiking poles, which we used to splint my leg, and with considerable support I was able to walk up the short, steep trail to the parking area. Coming down took about 10 minutes; the return trip probably took an hour. The patella is not a weight-bearing bone, so as long as I kept my leg fully extended the pain was bearable. I used a long sling under my foot to lift it when I had to climb over obstacles. From the parking area we drove to the local ER, where an X-ray revealed multiple fractures in the patella, entailing a later surgical repair.

ANALYSIS

I believe several factors contributed to this accident. First, and most important, there was not clear communication between me and my belayer. Normally I ask everyone I climb with to jump up if I fall, in order to give a dynamic belay. I weigh 115 pounds with my clothes on, so most people outweigh me—some significantly. So it's not difficult to give a dynamic belay, but the belayer has to be aware of the need for this. My belayer and I had climbed together for years, so I didn't think to stress that fact again.

Second, the belayer was using a Grigri. These are fantastic devices, but like anything else can be misapplied. I think that when I shouted I was coming off, the belayer sucked in the slack, which resulted in me arcing into the wall from a short distance above the bolt. When I asked the belayer why she didn't jump, she told me she thought I would hit the ground. I stopped at least 20 feet above the ground, so this was not a realistic concern. I have fallen on a number of the high-angle slabs at this

[Above] The appropriate amount of slack for belaying a sport climb varies with the terrain: less slack when ledge falls are possible and more slack (as shown here) to avoid short-roping a leader on an overhang. A good general guideline is to maintain a "gentle smile" of slack in the belay rope. *Courtesy of Dawn Glanc*

area with no problem in the past. The only ledge on this climb was near the first bolt, well below me. The one obstacle I was concerned about was the dihedral, which is why I jumped out (i.e. backward) to avoid hitting the lip when I fell. In my experience, a useful metric for leading goes like this:

• Before the first bolt, you will hit the ground if you fall.

• Between the first and second bolt, you may well hit the ground if the belayer isn't paying attention. This is probably the most dangerous area on the climb in terms of ground fall due to inattentive belaying. [*See Know the Ropes on page 14 for an illustration of this hazard.*]

• After the second bolt, depending on bolt spacing, the belayer can begin giving a softer catch by jumping up or moving in toward the wall if the leader falls. Of course, ledges are always a concern and require additional judgment from the belayer.

Good climbers and belayers always check each other: harness, knot, and belay device. I suggest an additional step: Before starting up, the leader should address his or her preferred belay techniques for the route. For example: "There is a ledge below the fourth bolt, so watch me close there." In my case, when the belayer's using a Grigri, I want a soft catch so I should request a short loop of slack or a jump. It's never good to assume your belayer is a mind reader. By spelling out the kind of catch you want, you're more likely to get it. (*Source: Beth Bennett.*)

[*Editor's note: In misguided efforts to give a "soft catch," some belayers leave a huge loop of slack in front of them as they belay sport climbs—or even pay out slack as the leader falls. These methods may only increase the impact of a fall, as well as the risk of hitting a ledge or other obstacle. In an article about this incident in* Rock & Ice *magazine, Alison Osius recommended belayers maintain a "gentle smile" of slack in the belay rope in front of them. A small arc of slack and a slight hop toward the first bolt are almost always sufficient to avoid short-roping the leader.*]

RAPPEL ERROR, STRANDED | FAILED TO FOLLOW DIRECTIONS
BOULDER, FIRST FLATIRON

On October 11, at approximately 7:15 p.m., several 911 calls came in to the City of Boulder Communications Center, stating that someone was yelling for help in the area of the First Flatiron. Temperatures at that time were in the low 50s (F), with light winds and clear skies. As emergency personnel began to stage near the base of the First

Flatiron, Open Space and Mountain Parks (OSMP) rangers were able to contact an involved person via his cell phone. This person, JG, was a member of a four-person climbing party, of which three were still on the summit. The leader of the climbing party, EW, had begun a rappel from the fixed eyebolt on the summit and had become stuck on the overhanging portion approximately 25 feet from the bottom of the 95-foot rappel. Due to the overhang and wind, those on the summit were unable to communicate effectively with EW. JG told rangers that he and his party on the summit had no headlamps, no food, and no additional clothing layers.

EW, 46, had a photocopy of route information from a guidebook that described three options for getting off the First Flatiron's summit: a single 95-foot rappel from the summit eyebolt; a short rappel from the summit and a second, slightly longer rappel from a bowl on the west face; or a low-fifth-class downclimb. EW mistakenly believed that all three options were steps in a single descent route.

When the party reached the summit at around dusk, EW tied two 60m ropes together, threaded them through the summit eyebolt, and threw both off the west face of the First Flatiron. One of the rappel ropes snagged on a flake about 50 feet above the ground when it was tossed from the summit, and in the darkness, without a headlamp, EW did not notice the problem until he had rappelled well below the flake, which caused the rope to jam in his belay device. EW knotted the free rope below his device to prevent any further descent, but he lacked prusiks, jumars, or any other means to travel back up his ropes.

Members of Rocky Mountain Rescue Group were able to lead up the nearby fifth-class descent route in the dark and reach the party stuck on the summit. Meanwhile, other personnel scrambled up the northwest face next to EW and built a high anchor and progress-capture system to pull the stuck climber over to the rock and conduct a "pick off" onto the rescuer's system. This successfully unloaded the jammed rappel line, which enabled the stuck climber to rappel to level ground. The other three members of the party and a Rocky Mountain Rescue member then used the previously stuck lines to rappel to the ground. The entire party was cold but uninjured.

Upon interview, EW stated he was an experienced trad climber (5.10/5.11), but had not been out regularly in several years, and had not climbed the First Flatiron in decades. EW said his group had begun their ascent of Fandango, a moderate multi-pitch route, at about noon and that he had led all of the pitches. Neither EW nor any other members of the party had anticipated how long it would take them to top out, and as a result had not brought sufficient equipment in the event they were benighted. (*Source: G. Frain, Ranger, City of Boulder Open Space and Mountain Parks.*)

ANALYSIS

The primary lessons from this incident are implicit in the report: 1) Get an early start for a long route; 2) research unfamiliar descents; and 3) carry the equipment necessary to ascend a rappel rope, particularly when making an unfamiliar rappel in the dark.

Every year many parties underestimate the length or difficulty of the 1,000-foot-plus east faces on Boulder's Flatirons. In March 2014, another party reached the summit of the First Flatiron after dark and was unable to rappel; rescuers reached them after 10:20 p.m. and assisted their descent. Another individual, a 22-year-old male, had to be rescued from the First Flatiron in February, after dark, after attempting to free solo the formation. Free soloing the Flatirons is popular, but the low-angle terrain can lure inexperienced climbers onto dangerous ground. In November a soloist fell from the 5.6 friction-slab crux of the direct east face of the First Flatiron, about 40 feet above the ground, and suffered serious injuries. (*Source: The Editors.*)

FALL ON ROCK | Off-Route, Inadequate Protection
BOULDER, THIRD FLATIRON

I was injured in a rock climbing accident on December 13. We were climbing Friday's Folly (5.7) on the back of the Third Flatiron. I've climbed the Third Flatiron probably over 100 times, but almost always soloing the East Face and either reversing the route or downclimbing the Southwest Chimney. I had never done Friday's or any adjacent routes. I was climbing with my friend Pat, and both of us have been climbing over 20 years. A route such as Friday's should be well within my comfort zone, and I led the first pitch with no problem. I established a belay at a fixed eyebolt at Friday's Folly Ledge, pulled up the remaining rope, and belayed Pat until he joined me.

Pat put me on belay and I went up and left from the bolt to start the second pitch. I saw what looked like a runout section above, didn't think it was a good idea for me that day, and downclimbed to the belay. I then went up and right into a dihedral with a wide crack. [*Editor's note: Friday's Folly is usually done as a single pitch, ending at the eyebolt about 75 feet up. There are two variations to the rarely climbed second pitch, and the right-hand version goes farther right than the line attempted by the author.*] The climbing started low angle, then steepened. I placed some gear, including a slung chockstone. I then placed a number 1 Camalot between a microwave-size block and the main wall—this was about a body length above the slung chockstone. I had poked and prodded the block and detected no motion. I yank-tested the cam, and it seemed stable, again with no motion.

The climbing overhead looked difficult: a steep, overhanging chimney or semi-cave, with some large, threatening boulders strewn within. It seemed significantly harder than 5.7, and not really like a "normal" route. I saw a potential line going to the left, with an overhanging section of rock forming a short offwidth section before the angle eased off. Again, it looked harder than 5.7, and I wasn't enthusiastic about falling on the cam beside the block. I could have downclimbed to the belay and explored other options or just rappelled to the ground. But I'm a bit of a stickler for climbing ethics or style: I thought it was a two-pitch climb, and I hadn't really "done" it until I did another pitch.

I thought that if I attached a sling to the cam and stood in it, maybe I could reach handholds that would allow me to climb left across the offwidth. I decided to "take" before attaching the sling. I yelled "take" to Pat, then "take tight." Here's where things really went wrong. I saw the cam pull out of the rock and the chockstone coming toward me. I remember thinking "oh shit" and that I should try to avoid the falling chockstone as I fell. According to Pat, I fell 15 to 20 feet, slamming into the slabby terrain below as the rope caught at the slung chockstone. The block I had pulled out drove into my back and then shattered on a ledge, sending fragments to the ground. Fortunately, Pat was well to the left and wasn't hit.

I was knocked out. My lack of motion suggested to Pat that I was dead or nearly so. He yelled for help. Perhaps surprisingly to him, I regained consciousness after some seconds, moaning and communicating in grunts and broken words. Pat was able to lower me to near his belay point, but I was too far to the side to be lowered directly to him. I was bleeding from a head wound. Not as obvious, but significant: My back was broken, and my left shoulder and upper arm were wrecked. And some minor issues: a small liver laceration, smashed thumb, and miscellaneous cuts and bruises. Luckily, the broken back was just a broken bone—no neurological damage. The head wound was mostly superficial.

[Above] The First, Second, and Third Flatirons (right to left). Climbers frequently underestimate the size of these 1,000-foot-plus faces. *Dougald MacDonald*

I was able to swing close enough for Pat to grab me and secure me to the bolt. We're taught not to move people with possible spinal cord issues, and Pat could have waited with me for rescuers to arrive, or he could have left me attached to the bolt while he rappelled to the ground. But Pat made the decision to get me to the ground as quickly as reasonably possible. My head injury looked very serious, and it appeared that I might have significant internal injuries. He thought my total condition required getting treatment ASAP.

Pat rigged a chest harness and got me into a tolerably comfortable position to be lowered. Once I was on the ground, he fixed the rope to the bolt, and rappelled. I recall increasing consciousness and pain. Some guy in the area gave me warm clothes and encouragement. The Rocky Mountain Rescue Group appeared in about 45 minutes, as dusk settled in.

I'm not the best person to give an account of the rescue—I got a lovely view of the sky as it turned from gray to black, and of the often sweat-drenched faces of the many hardworking rescuers who rotated turns carrying and lowering the litter. Eventually we made it to an ambulance and then to Boulder Community Hospital. It looks like I will make a good recovery.

ANALYSIS

I was not wearing my helmet. The helmet-averse who read this can learn from my mistake. Consider that I lost consciousness from impact—always serious—and that it easily could have been worse. A helmet also may have allowed me to participate more actively in the rescue and help Pat evaluate whether immediate lowering was the right action. Risk-taking in partnered rope climbing affects both climbers. There is a saying: You don't have to wear a helmet, but I don't have to belay you either.

Every accident may suggest various preventive measures, from the overly general ("Don't rock climb") to the overly specific ("Don't climb the second pitch of Friday's Folly"). I'm still processing this one, but my main advice is to be super-careful with loose rock and ultra-careful when your protection interacts with loose rock. (*Source: Peter Weinberg.*)

INADEQUATE BELAY

BOULDER

After 29 years of accident-free climbing, I thought I was a pretty competent belayer. Turns out I still had plenty to learn. Luckily I'm still accident-free, but things easily could have ended very badly.

This happened when I was lowering my friend Kevin off a lead climb at a local climbing gym. It's a scenario they warn you about in the pamphlets that come with carabiners and belay devices, but until now I'd thought it was just a theoretical possibility that wouldn't happen in the real world. I was using my usual setup: a Black Diamond ATC and a Petzl William locking biner. The William is a sturdy screw-gate biner with a nice wide gate, but it sometimes slips into a cross-loaded position, which is what happened this time.

As far as Kevin and I can figure out, here's what happened next: The rope was running against the carabiner's locking sleeve and caused it to rotate into the unlocked position as I lowered Kevin. Then the edge of the ATC pushed against the gate and caused it to open slightly. The rope slipped into the gap and popped out of the biner. The carabiner gate closed again, leaving the ATC in place but nothing holding the rope.

I didn't actually see this happen because I was looking up at Kevin the whole time. All I knew was that suddenly there was a hard pull on the rope. The saving graces were (A) Kevin's pretty light; (B) there was lots of friction in the system because the rope was running through eight quickdraws; (C) my brake hand was firmly on the rope and

[Left] A belayer's screw-gate carabiner was unlocked by the action of the rope as he lowered his climbing partner. **[Right]** The rope then popped out of the open gate. *Erik Rieger*

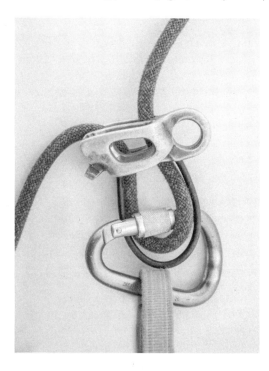
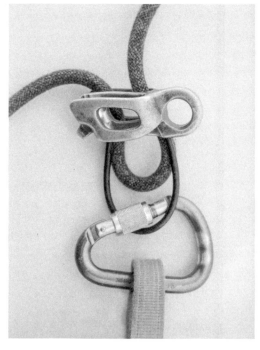

instinctively I was able to hold it tight, even before I realized what was happening; and (D) I didn't have to lower Kevin very far.

Kevin was really good about the whole thing. He seemed more concerned about a minor rope burn on my hand than the fact that he'd narrowly escaped serious injury. On my way home I stopped at REI and bought a BD Gridlock biner, which won't easily slip into a cross-loaded position. (*Source: Martin le Roux.*)

ANALYSIS

As the author describes, this is rare scenario but it can indeed happen. A two- or three-stage locking device on the carabiner (versus a screw gate) could prevent this, as could orienting the gate of the locking carabiner on the opposite side of the brake hand. However, neither of these techniques will prevent cross-loading, which can direct the forces of a fall onto the weakest parts of the carabiner. Several models of locking belay carabiners are designed specifically to prevent cross-loading. It's also important to develop a habit of glancing down at your belay system periodically to make sure everything looks correct. (*Source: The Editors.*)

FALL ON ROCK | Lead Rope Unclipped From Protection

ELDORADO CANYON STATE PARK, LOWER PEANUTS WALL

Shortly after noon on Saturday, August 9, Wayne Crill (46 at the time) was attempting to lead a new route on the left side of Lower Peanuts Wall. He was belayed by Greg Miller. Crill and Miller had previously worked the route on top-rope, figuring out the moves and assessing the number and quality of protection opportunities. According to Miller, they knew a few points of protection were of marginal quality, but they felt that even if those points failed in a fall, the sounder protection placements would prevent a ground fall.

During his lead attempt, Crill had placed seven pieces of protection over about the first 30 feet of the climb. The line shifted slightly left to right a few times, but at about 30 feet up, Crill was more or less straight above the start of the climb. From that point, he climbed diagonally up and right about 10 feet and placed another piece. He clipped a 21-inch, 8mm Dyneema sling into this piece. The sling likely had been triple-looped on his rack, so he would have clipped it into the piece of protection, unclipped the bottom carabiner, extended the sling, and, presumably, clipped the lead rope into the bottom carabiner. The top carabiner on the sling had a wire gate, and most likely the lower carabiner also had a wire gate.

From here, Crill climbed diagonally up and right about another 10 feet, placed another piece of protection, and used a similarly equipped 21-inch sling in a similar manner. (Miller has stated that Crill may also have placed another point of protection between these two pieces.) Now Crill climbed straight up, about another 10 feet, and placed a slider nut and a stopper equipped with a "screamer" for a quickdraw.

According to Miller, Crill was almost to an obvious undercling, just below the roof band that diagonals up and right across the wall, when he fell. The stopper pulled, but not before a few of the bar tacks on the screamer ripped (as they are designed to do to reduce the force of a fall.) The slider nut also pulled. The fifth piece of protection that Crill had placed was pulled out by the action of the rope. And, if there had been a placement between Crill's eighth and ninth pieces, as Miller suggests, it also pulled.

As improbable as it sounds, what also seems to have happened is that the force of the fall, likely exacerbated by vibration and slack created by the gear that failed, caused the rope-end carabiners on both of Crills' eighth and ninth pieces (along the diagonal traverse) to unclip from their respective slings. That left the high point of the rope as the seventh piece of protection that Crill had placed. This piece was too low to arrest the fall, and he fell all the way to the ground.

Responding to screams for help and telephone calls, park rangers, Rocky Mountain Rescue personnel, a sheriff's deputy, and ambulance personnel arrived on scene. Crill was unconscious and bleeding from the head. Rescuers stabilized him, loaded him into a litter, and lowered him down the talus slope below Lower Peanuts Wall to the Fowler Trail. The litter was placed on a wheel, and the victim was transported to an ambulance waiting at the trailhead. Soon afterward, Crill was loaded into a helicopter and transported to a hospital.

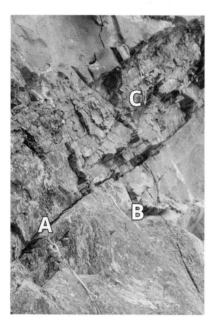

[Above] The leader fell at least 10 feet above piece C. His rope somehow unclipped from the long slings on pieces C and B, leaving A as his highest protection. He fell to the ground. *Eldorado Canyon State Park*

ANALYSIS

Responders' initial on-scene efforts were directed to stabilizing and packaging Crill for evacuation. After the rescue, the stopper (with screamer attached) and slider nut, and two free carabiners (both with wire gates), were found at the scene. The rope ran up through the first seven protection placements and back down to the ground. (The fifth placement had pulled from the rock but was held up by the fourth protection placement.) Above the seventh placement and the high point of the rope, 21-inch slings were clipped to the eighth and ninth pieces, with no carabiners at the bottom of each of the slings.

Though not at all common, there are two ways this can occur. Carabiner gates can flutter open when a carabiner violently bangs against the rock, or simply by vibrations created when arresting a fall. This may be more likely to cause carabiner failure, rather than unclipping, because a closed gate is critical to the full strength of the carabiner. It is also possible with an open loop of sling, where the rope-end carabiner doesn't have a mechanism to secure it in place (such as a sewn loop or clove hitch), for the sling to twist and the carabiner to orient itself in such a way that the gate slams against a side of the sling, opens up, and the carabiner unclips from the sling. In this particular case, the very rare event of a carabiner unclipping from a sling happened not once but twice. (*Source: Eldorado Canyon State Park incident report, written by Steve Muehlhauser, Ranger.*)

(*Editor's note: As Muehlhauser suggests in his report, fixing the rope-end carabiner to the sling with a clove hitch or other method might prevent it from twisting around a sling and unclipping. However, knots weaken thin Dyneema slings. The surest way to prevent a carabiner gate from vibrating or banging open—or from unclipping itself against a sling— is to use a locking carabiner. For crucial placements, this can provide an extra measure of security. In Crill's case, where two separate placements came unclipped, extremely bad luck played a major role. He was wearing a helmet, which may have mitigated his injuries. Nonetheless, he suffered a traumatic brain injury. Ten months after the accident, his recovery continued to progress.)*

FALL ON ROCK | Miscommunication
ELDORADO CANYON STATE PARK, WEST RIDGE

In the late afternoon on October 19, a party of four was climbing on the West Ridge in two parties of two. According to one of these climbers, Mark Hanna, a male climber, 42, and his partner were top-roping the first pitch of Iron Horse (5.11) as their last climb of the day. The climber topped out at the anchors, about 80 feet above the ground, and yelled "OK!" At this point his belayer took him off belay, thinking the climber would descend via rappel, as they had done on previous climbs throughout the day. The climber leaned back to be lowered and fell about 60 feet to a ledge 15 to 20 feet off the ground. He was caught by a small juniper. A climber on scene scrambled up, secured him, and tried to keep him comfortable until Rocky Mountain Rescue arrived.

The climber regained consciousness after a few minutes and was able to talk and answer questions, which was a positive sign considering he was not wearing his helmet. His injuries included a bad scalp laceration and multiple fractures (leg, heel, and pelvis). He was evacuated by helicopter. (*Source: Mark Hanna.*)

ANALYSIS

This is an all-too-common type of accident. Before starting a climb, the belayer and climber must clearly agree on what the climber plans to do when he or she reaches the anchors. The belayer should never take the climber off until he is certain the climber is off belay. The climber also needs to be precise with instructions once he reaches the anchor. If this climber had yelled "take" or "lower" instead of "OK," it would have made it clearer to the belayer that he was ready to be lowered instead of planning to rappel. The climber also should test the system and, if possible, visually verify that he's still on belay before trusting that he's ready to be lowered. (*Source: The Editors.*)

FALL FROM TYROLEAN | Faulty Use of Equipment
CLEAR CREEK CANYON, EAST COLFAX

On April 9, I had been clipping bolts at East Colfax with Mike Endicott, Leo Paik, Dave Rogers, and Doug Redosh. Mike and I decided to cross Clear Creek to climb at some other crags. The creek was too deep to wade, so an established double-rope Tyrolean traverse provided the obvious choice. The proximal ends of the ropes were attached to a small tree that leaned toward the creek over an eroding embankment.

Mike went first, commenting that clipping into the ropes for the traverse felt like 5.10. After he crossed the creek, I climbed the tree from the south side, as Mike did, and hung from a branch stub with my left hand as I struggled to clip in to the Silent Partner that I had placed on top of the ropes (which were now positioned below me). I had routinely used the Silent Partner as a double-rope pulley for smooth rides across Tyrolean traverses.

After succeeding in clipping my belay loop to the Silent Partner, I moved it back and forth along the ropes, noting that the sheave (the device's main drum or wheel)

[Left] A Silent Partner broken when it was inappropriately used as a pulley and flipped upside-down. Always back up your attachment to a Tyrolean traverse. *George Bracksieck*

was above the ropes. However, I didn't recognize that the locking-carabiner attachment point was also above the ropes, and that when I let go of the tree and swung down, the device would flip and the sheave now would be *under* the ropes. This loaded the end of the Silent Partner that is only closed with two slim retaining rods. These broke under my weight, the device blew off the ropes, and I fell about 10 feet onto the edge of a slab, landing on my upper left femur. On a scale of one to ten, the pain level was at 12. I tumbled down over small boulders to the edge of the creek. I was instinctively preparing to swim, while thinking that I wouldn't be able to kick. The impact shattered the femur into many pieces and blew it out of the hip socket.

ANALYSIS

The main lesson is to use a backup. If I had simply clipped a shoulder-length sling (or anchor tether) from my harness to the ropes, I would have ended up dangling from the ropes and not on the ground. My helmet and pack provided protection from other potential injuries. This wasn't a climbing accident. I fell from a tree instead of rock. Perhaps this should be written up for Accidents in North American Forestry. (*Source: George Bracksieck.*)

[*Editor's note: The author, age 64 at the time of this incident, is a highly experienced climber. As he says above, he had used this device as a pulley many times. However, the manufacturer, Rock Exotica, states that the Silent Partner is designed as a self-belay device for leading and top-roping and should not be used for any other purpose, and also that the rope must be loaded into the device with a clove hitch tied around the device's central drum. The manufacturer does not recommend using it as a pulley.*]

FALL ON ROCK | Inexperience, Faulty Use of Equipment
STAUNTON STATE PARK, TAN CORRIDOR

I heard a scream and saw my rope falling below me. It was August 23, the day I almost died. After putting in six hours of rock climbing, we were ready to pack up and leave the Tan Corridor. I (Asha Nanda, 21) started up the climb called Reef On It to break down the anchor of our last climb. It was a 5.10- that Douglas Sargent Kern had led earlier in the day and left up for me to top-rope.

I got to the top, clipped into the anchor, and sat back in my harness to test my weight. "Off belay!" I called down to my belayer, Julie MacCready. I had clipped in with a single alpine draw, a sling with a carabiner taped into place at one end like a quickdraw. This supported my full weight from above as I leaned back and focused on setting up the rappel. As I was threading the rope back through the anchor, I felt myself falling. I experienced the rawest form of terror as the air whipped past, the wind carrying my scream to the ground. Startled by the scream, MacCready looked up to see my body plummeting downward. Kern jumped up and ran forward to try to catch me. With arms open and feet spread apart, he braced himself for the impact as my 125-pound body fell from about 60 feet up. I hit him in the chest and arms before bouncing onto the boulders and rolling a few feet.

I was flat on the ground, my back pressed against the rocks. Kern and Jennifer Lee immediately began assessing me for damage. MacCready dialed 911, while Erika Bannon, a climber who had seen the whole accident, ran down the mountain to guide rescuers to the scene. What seemed like only minutes later, Elk Creek Fire Department arrived with a large rescue party. They treated me for shock and loaded me onto a stretcher to carry me down the trail. I was taken to a landing zone and airlifted to a hospital in Denver, arriving two hours after the fall.

Seven hours later, a miracle was confirmed. No internal bleeding, concussion, or broken bones—every scan, test, and X-ray had come back negative. The medical staff was in awe. When my nurse heard what Kern had done, she shook her head in disbelief. "If he had not broken your fall, you could have died or at best ended up paralyzed for life." I walked out of that ER late that night with only bruises and scratches to show for my six-story freefall. When Kern is asked how he reacted with such speed and remained standing after the impact he states, "God is good."

ANALYSIS

Never tape slings to create quickdraws. Always have redundant tethers to anchors. If you're new to climbing, advance cautiously and with respect for the risks. (*Source: Asha Nanda.*)

[*Editor's note: A similar incident occurred in the New River Gorge (2010). In this case, a Petzl String was installed at the ends of two slings along with locking carabiners. (The String is a rubber "keeper" designed to fit on the end of a quickdraw or runner in order to keep*

[Left] Some climbers tape slings to hold the carabiners in place. **[Middle]** However, if a loop of the sling gets caught inside the carabiner, as shown, only the tape will be holding the sling in place. **[Right]** If the sling is weighted and the tape breaks, the sling will pull right out of the carabiner. *Dougald MacDonald*

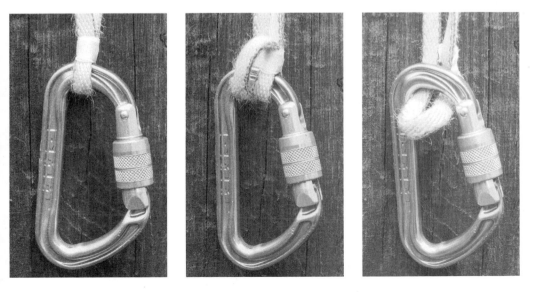

the lower carabiner in place for easy clipping and to protect the webbing from abrasion). After this accident a local climber climbed to the anchor and found a locking carabiner on each bolt with a String still affixed to each. Both Strings were torn on the side. Search "The Danger of Open Quickdraws" for an excellent short video from UKClimbing.com illustrating how such "alpine draws" can come unclipped.]

CONNECTICUT

FALL ON ROCK, NUT PULLED OUT | No Helmet
RAGGED MOUNTAIN, SMALL CLIFF

On April 30 I was leading Diagonal (5.6) on the Small Cliff at Ragged Mountain. I fell from about halfway up, at a point where the diagonaling crack offsets to the right. I had put in a cam about 10 feet up and then a nut in a not-great placement. I was looking for another placement, holding a sloping hold, and my foot must have slipped. I pulled out my second piece, which was in an expanding crack, and the next moment I was on my back on the trail. There was a rock among the leaves, resulting in the ribs on my back right side being broken in 10 places. I also had a laceration on the top of my head that required six stitches. I was airlifted to a hospital in Hartford.

ANALYSIS

I was familiar with the climb and had led it many times, although not recently. A more secure placement for the nut and a helmet would have turned this fall into merely an embarrassing incident during an otherwise beautiful spring day. (*Source: Sam Streibert.*)

IDAHO

FALL ON ROCK
CITY OF ROCKS, ELEPHANT ROCK

On May 24, a climber in his early 20s was leading Rye Crisp (5.8) while his sister belayed him. According to his sister, he was an experienced climber who leads up to 5.11. Because the climb was relatively easy for him, he had not placed any protection, though there was ample opportunity to do so. Approximately 40 feet up, his foot slipped and he fell to the ground, landing on a granite slab on his left elbow. The elbow was severely broken. Climbing ranger Brad Shilling and four other climbers, all wilderness first responders, assisted the climber, placed him on a backboard, and evacuated him to a waiting ambulance.

ANALYSIS

A slip can happen at any time, no matter how experienced you are. If you have protection with you (as he did) there's no reason not to use it. (*Source: Anonymous responder at the accident scene.*)

KENTUCKY

FALL ON ROCK, BELAYER ERROR
MUIR VALLEY, TECTONIC WALL

During the early evening on Saturday, October 4, a female climber (20) was leading the sport route Plate Tectonics (5.9). When she was between the second and third bolt, about 26 feet off the ground, she fell. Neither the climber nor the belayer was wearing a helmet. The climber impacted the ground, hitting first on her feet then falling back onto her butt. Observers reported that she freefell with no significant arresting from her rope.

The belayer, a 20-year-old female, was observed to be inattentive to her climber and using poor belay technique with an ATC. Several climbers close to the scene reported that, at the time of the fall, the belayer was holding the rope with both hands up above the belay device in a such a way that no bight of rope was formed over the lip of the ATC. When the falling climber pulled the slack out of the rope, it simply continued to pay out through the belay device until she hit the ground. The climber sustained non-life-threatening injuries to her back, pelvis, and feet.

Bystanders ran to the nearest Muir Valley Emergency Radio Station and called for help. Within four minutes, Muir Valley Rescue (MVR) personnel were on scene. MVR volunteers assisted in treating, packaging, and transporting the victim in a litter to a

[Below] Belaying with the brake hand held high (left) provides limited braking force for catching a leader fall. A well-prepared belayer (right) keeps the brake hand low whenever possible, ready to catch a sudden fall with maximum braking power. *Rick Weber*

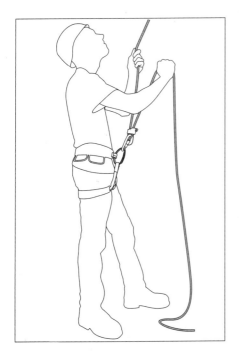 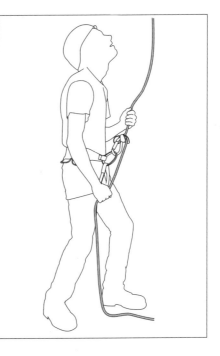

waiting ambulance on Muir's Emergency Road. From there, she was transported by ambulance to a nearby medical facility for further treatment.

ANALYSIS

This is a classic mistake made by inexperienced belayers that can be simply summed up: no bight, no brake. Oddly, this two-hands-above-the-ATC technique is sometimes taught in climbing gyms. Because many beginning gym climbers are on a top-rope, they don't generate the force in a fall that a lead climber does, and the belayer can usually arrest the fall even without forming the bight with the brake hand. When the belayer needs to catch a much bigger load with a falling leader, the sloppy technique can fail. (*Source: Rick Weber, Muir Valley.*)

[*Editor's note: According to Rick Weber, more than 40,000 climbers visited Muir Valley during 2014. In addition to the incident reported here, there were six other emergency calls that required first aid and trips to the ER, but were relatively minor in nature. One other climber experienced a severe but non-life-threatening injury when he fumbled a clip and fell with the rope coiled around his thumb and index finger, causing an avulsion of the finger and part of his thumb. The digit fragments were found right below the climb, kept cool with a cold pack—and then on ice in the ambulance—and brought to the hospital with the climber. The digits were successfully reimplanted, allowing the climber, a surgeon, to return to work and climbing at full strength.*]

FALL ON ROCK, LOWERING ERROR | Rope Too Short
RED RIVER GORGE, MOTHERLODE

On September 26 I fell about 40 feet while lowering from a session on the Madness (5.13c), which I was hoping might be my 1,500th route in the Red River Gorge. Once I realized I was falling, I cursed, straightened up, got my feet underneath me, and had just enough time to think "feet shoulder width apart, knees bent, back straight, head up" before my feet hit the ground. This was essential to my "successful" landing.

My knees struck my chest and knocked my breath away. I crumpled into a ball on the ground. When I opened my eyes I saw that my right arm was facing the wrong way, and that there were two rocks on either side of my head that I had somehow narrowly missed. Since the arm wasn't painful yet, I grabbed the flopping hand, paired up the bones, and set it into place. I tried to hold it there while attempting to roll onto my side. Neither operation was successful. The arm sprang back into its previously backward position, and I was still lying on my chest. Now I was in a lot of pain. I was pretty sure something in my back was broken. Luckily, someone at the crag that day had a satellite phone and the local rescue squad was called right away. They arrived surprisingly soon afterward.

As it turns out, my back was indeed fractured, my arm was broken, and my elbow was chipped. I was non-ambulatory, so the local rescue squad, along with my friends, carried me out in a Stokes basket, just as I had carried out many before during my rescue career. It was a humbling and embarrassing experience.

ANALYSIS

Sometimes it is a big dumb mistake that causes an accident and sometimes, as in this case, it can happen after several small safety procedures are missed. I had chosen a fat older rope as I began to work the moves on the Madness, without taking into account that I had cut worn-out sections from this rope a couple of times. I had even used this this very rope on the Madness, but I'd never gotten all the way to the anchors with it. When I transferred this rope from one tarp to another, I overlooked tying both ends of the rope to the tarp.

A 70-meter rope is required for this route, and I estimate I'd previously cut five or six meters from each end. During the descent, I was talking to my belayer, discussing how optimistic I was regarding the route. At about 40 feet from the ground, I reached for the top of a small tree to turn myself in the air and face the cliff. My belayer was listening to me and watching me reach for the tree when the end of the rope shot through his belay device. Although my partner and I had over 52 years of combined climbing experience, experience isn't always enough. The importance of following safety procedures cannot be overemphasized:

1) Use appropriate equipment. Make sure the rope is long enough to ascend and descend the route you are climbing.

2) Close the system. Tie a stopper knot, tie into a rope bag, or tie into your belayer.

3) Pay attention while belaying. The climber's safety is your responsibility from the second his feet leave the ground until he is safely back on terra firma.

4) Hold your brake hand on the rope well away from an assisted-braking belay device. If the rope were to slip through your hand, there still might be a chance the device would lock on the leftover rope.

5) Be prepared. Get medical training, know your surroundings, and carry a cell/sat phone that works where you are, if possible. (*Source: Blake Bowling.*)

[Below] White line marks the Madness (5.13c) at the Motherlode. X marks the approximate spot where the climber began falling because his rope was too short. *Blake Bowling*

MONTANA

FALL ON ROCK | Climbing Unroped
BITTERROOT NATIONAL FOREST, BLODGETT CANYON

Ryan Silsby, 25, died in a fall in Blodgett Canyon in mid-August. Silsby had parked at the Blodgett Canyon Trailhead, planning a two-day trip. His vehicle was found on September 2 with his camping gear still inside it, and his body was discovered on September 7 at the base of a rock formation on the south side of the canyon, about half a mile from the trailhead, after climbers spotted his pack. He had been free soloing and likely fell on August 16 or 17, the coroner determined.

ANALYSIS

Telling someone exactly where you're going when climbing alone can dramatically speed searches, especially in remote locations. In this case, it would not have changed the outcome for the climber, but it would have spared his family and friends some anguish. (*Source: The Editors.*)

NEW HAMPSHIRE

FALL ON ROCK | Rope Soloing
CATHEDRAL LEDGE, BARBER WALL

At approximately 11:40 a.m. on July 12, I greeted a solo climber as I was rappelling Chicken Delight on the Barber Wall at Cathedral Ledge with a client. I observed that the solo climber had just rappelled Double Vee/Jolt on a static line, and appeared to be preparing to rope-solo back up, using an ascender rigged to a chest harness as an auto-belay. I also observed a party of two on the nearby climb Nutcracker.

I short-roped my client, J.M., over to the climb Upper Refuse, which is a couple of hundred yards away from the Barber Wall and out of sight. I had just started leading Upper Refuse when one of the climbers who had been on Nutcracker appeared below and asked if anyone was an EMT, as a climber had fallen 70 feet and was seriously injured. I asked if 911 had been called, and he confirmed he was on the phone with them. I left a piece of protection in the climb and quickly downclimbed back to J.M. I then pulled my rope and short-roped J.M. back to the accident scene.

I arrived at the base of the Barber Wall at 12:12 p.m., about 12 minutes after the fall. The victim, B.D., was conscious when I arrived, but the two witnesses confirmed he had been unconscious for at least five minutes after the fall. He had come to rest crumpled around a tree, with his head downhill. I immediately noticed what appeared to be a left femur fracture, as well as some trauma to his face. I found no signs of a head injury on the back of the victim's head, even though he was not wearing a helmet.

B.D. was able to communicate his name, age, residence, and where he was, but not what month it was. In order to put traction on the left femur, I had the two recreational climbers and my client aid me by supporting his head and arms while we straightened him into a position where I could get traction on his leg and look for other life-threatening injuries. Once I found no other immediate threats, I called Mountain Rescue Service to update them on the severity of the victim's injuries and confirm they knew exactly where we were (since 911 sometimes does not relay an accurate location).

During my secondary exam I discovered an open tear in the victim's lower right arm, where it appeared he had sustained an open compound fracture and the bone had reduced on its own. The 10-inch laceration was not bleeding much, so I put slight traction on that arm, which eased the pain. B.D. also complained of his right leg hurting, and while there was no obvious fracture we applied slight traction on that leg, which seemed to lower his pain.

Over the next 50 minutes the victim stayed "AOx2" (alert and aware of name and location). He continuously complained of difficulty breathing and confusion about what had happened. Two sets of vitals recorded a heart rate of 100 and difficulty breathing. A couple of other climbers had arrived, and I facilitated a rotation of people applying manual traction, giving each person an opportunity to stand and rest. I continually checked on my client, J.M., who was steadfast while we cared for B.D.

[Above] A climber on Double Vee at Cathedral Ledge. The solo climber who fell here had anchored his ropes above this route and above Jolt, just to the left. He may have mistakenly clipped his rappel device to the slack rope between the two anchors. *Lucie Parietti*

At 12:50 p.m. a Mountain Rescue Service member made contact with me from the top of the Barber Wall, and 15 minutes later the paramedics arrived. The lead paramedic took over medical care, and I redirected my focus on scene safety as we now had non-climber paramedics on scene, with questionable footing where they were accessing the victim. I anchored the one who appeared to be the least sure-footed and most exposed, then started gathering our gear for the carry-out.

Mountain Rescue Service had set up a traversing hand line as well as a belay line for the litter, in order to facilitate the carry-out in third-class terrain. While stopped at a rope-switch point, I noticed the victim staring at the sun and placed my hands to shade his eyes. His pupils were unresponsive. The lead paramedic was notified that the patient's condition had changed, and he made a few last-ditch efforts before calling him "coded." As rigor had started to set in, and the cause of death was likely severe internal trauma, no CPR was performed. The time was approximately 1:50 p.m.

ANALYSIS

Because the victim was climbing alone, I can only speculate on what happened, based on the evidence I saw. When I arrived no one had touched the victim. He had a single strand of static rope threaded through an ATC and clipped with a locking carabiner to his belay loop. The carabiner was locked. His ascender, clipped to an improvised chest harness, was not attached to a rope. He had another locking carabiner on his belay loop that was not in use. There was a fair amount of slack in the rope on both sides of the belay device.

I confirmed from the Mountain Rescue Service member who had arrived at the top of the cliff that one end of B.D.'s rope was anchored to a tree above Double Vee with a bowline, and then redirected off another tree, presumably to position the rope over Jolt. The other end of the rope was unsecured at the top of the cliff, leaving a "loop" that hung down to where the victim came to rest. The nearby climbers said his fall had started from the very top of the cliff.

From this info I speculate that B.D. rappelled a single strand of his static rope to the base of Jolt. He then used his chest-rigged ascender to self-belay an ascent of Jolt. At the top of the climb he removed the ascender and installed his belay/rappel device on the rope, but he appears to have attached the device to the wrong point on the rope, with 70-plus feet of slack between it and the anchor. He then leaned back to descend. Another theory is that an unknown medical condition caused him let go of his brake hand while rappelling, but the fact that there was a fair amount of slack in the system where he came to rest doesn't really support this. It's also possible he had left the ATC on the rope while ascending Jolt, then pulled up all the rope after removing his ascender, and then somehow fell, with the free end of the rope somehow getting caught at the top of the cliff. [*The top of the Barber Wall is non-technical but because of the dense conifer growth on Cathedral Ledge, pine needles make it easy to slip, especially in rock shoes.*] None of these scenarios would be forgiving, as there is a vertical, 70-foot fall to a flat ledge.

It should be noted that B.D., age 56, was a well-known New England climber with experience spanning three decades, across the country, and countless hard first ascents to his name. The list of renowned climbers that knew and trusted him as a safe and extremely competent climber is long. (*Source: D.G. Lottmann, Mountain Rescue Service member.*)

NEW YORK

FALL ON ROCK | Inadequate Protection, Cam Pulled Out
SHAWANGUNKS, THE TRAPPS, CASCADING CRYSTAL KALEIDOSCOPE

On August 9 a climber was starting either the second pitch of Cascading Crystal Kaleidoscope (CCK) or CCK Direct—the pitches start in the same area of Grand Traverse Ledge. He reportedly placed one cam in a horizontal crack, continued climbing, decided to retreat, and then fell or "took" on the cam. The piece popped and he fell 15 to 20 feet onto Grand Traverse Ledge, suffering a broken back and incomplete spinal cord injury. Rescuers lowered him and carried him to the Carriage Road, and he was airlifted to a hospital. Initially the climber was paralyzed from the waist down, but after surgery and rehab he has recovered significantly and is able to walk.

ANALYSIS

Many routes at the Gunks require calculated risks and run-outs, and CCK is a good example. The two main options for leaving Grand Traverse Ledge (5.7+ and 5.8+) both are considered PG/R for seriousness. If a climber is in doubt about this pitch, an easier and well-protected alternative (Updraft, 5.5) leads to a belay stance from which the final pitch of CCK or CCK Direct is easily accessed. Cam placements are prone to walking in horizontal cracks, and extending the piece with a long sling may prevent this. When making crucial protection placements (a single piece protecting against a long fall), backing up the piece is always recommended. (*Source: The Editors.*)

FALL ON ROCK | No Protection

SHAWANGUNKS, THE TRAPPS, YELLOW WALL

Heidi Duartes Wahl, 28, died November 15 after falling to the ground from about 20 feet up Yellow Wall (5.11) at the Trapps. The climber had not placed any protection, which is the norm for the relatively easy but poorly protected start of this route. She appears to have broken her neck in the groundfall and died at the scene or soon afterward. She was wearing a helmet.

ANALYSIS

A Chilean climber living in the United States, Duartes Wahl was highly experienced and skilled. She appears to have slipped on relatively easy ground (approximately 5.7 on a 5.11 climb) before she reached good protection. This tragic accident points up the potentially catastrophic consequences of a short fall onto the ground or a ledge, and thus the need for great care even on terrain that is very easy for the climber. (*Source: The Editors.*)

NORTH CAROLINA

FALL ON ROCK | Rope Soloing

CROWDERS MOUNTAIN STATE PARK, MIDDLE FINGER WALL

Mark Byers (53), an experienced climber, died as a result of a fall while roped solo climbing on the evening of March 11. Byers was leading the route Balcony (5.5). Witnesses mistakenly reported that he had reached the top of the climb and that one of his anchors pulled, causing him to fall. The witnesses reported he fell about 60 feet, striking his head against the rock several times. His rope prevented him from hitting the ground, leaving him on a ledge 10 to 15 feet up. He was not breathing and did not have a pulse when paramedics reached him.

ANALYSIS

In an attempt to shed some light on the event, Bradley Woolf, Robert Hutchins, and I met with park staff to examine the scene. The park had collected some of Mark's belongings, including his harness (cut by rescuers), his Soloist self-belay device (still secured to the belay loop), his chest sling (cut by rescuers), and the section of rope

[Above] The Soloist belay device was not designed to hold inverted falls.

that was trailing from his harness. Rescuers cut his rope to extract him. Tellingly, there was an overhand knot proximal to the cut end of the rope. This suggests that Mark's Soloist did not engage during his fall and that the backup knot is what prevented him from falling to the ground.

We accompanied park staff to the climb and found no signs of broken gear at the base. Looking up, we could clearly see an intact anchor at the first-pitch belay ledge for the Balcony (about 50 feet up) and a rope tied there and extending up the cliff to an unseen high piece of gear. From the unseen gear the rope descended to a point about 15 feet above the base (some distance below the belay anchor). At the cliff top there was no sign of damage to the existing bolt anchors, and there was no sign that Mark had in fact even reached the top.

Bradley and I rappelled to inspect Mark's high piece. Approximately 40 feet from the lip we found an intact number 7 stopper clipped into the rope with a sling. This is the piece that held Mark's fall.

We rappelled down to the anchor we had seen from the ground. It consisted of two 0.5 Camalots and a pink Tricam equalized with a cordelette. There was a red Tricam hanging from the anchor, but not a part of it. We agreed that this was a directional or an early piece of gear placed as Mark led out from his belay anchor. This placement likely failed due to a lateral pull from the rope as Mark fell, but had little bearing on the distance he fell. Above the red Tricam we found a sling girth-hitched around a rock feature. This sling was still clipped into the rope. From here the rope was clipped into the previously described high gear. Above the highest piece the route steepens and pulls through a bulge. We found fresh chalk here, but no sign of broken rock.

After our site visit, our group felt very confident the accident was not a product of gear failure but rather the result of an inverted fall that caused the Soloist self-belay device to fail to engage. It is highly likely that while pulling the bulge Mark fell into an inverted body orientation. It is also possible that falling with the rope behind his leg could have inverted Mark. Either way, falling upside-down can cause the Soloist device to fail to engage, a possibility the former manufacturer warned users about.

Rescuers report that Mark's airway was compromised by a chest sling he was wearing and that this was likely the proximal cause of death. Pictures that Mark took during a prior ascent show a red sling configured such that the tie-in point was in the center of his chest (secured with locking carabiner). This effectively creates an X across the front of the chest, which could ride up in the event of a fall and impact the victim's airway.

In summary, site evidence and the knot in the rope suggest that Mark took a leader fall while climbing through the steepest part of the route. This fall was not arrested by the Soloist, probably because of his body orientation. Once the fall was stopped by the backup knot, Mark's chest rig rode up on his torso to the point where it impacted his airway. Perhaps due to his injuries, Mark was unable to right himself and take weight off the chest sling. (*Source: Eddie Medina, Carolina Climbers Coalition.*)

[*Editor's note: The Soloist belay device is no longer manufactured. Climbers who still use this device must be aware that it is only designed to catch a leader falling in a relatively upright position. Consider appropriate backups*.]

FALL ON ROCK | Rockfall, Failure to Test Hold
PISGAH NATIONAL FOREST, VICTORY WALL

On March 21, MT (30) and her partner (age 35) started an unnamed 5.7/5.8 climb on the Victory Wall. MT began the second pitch by moving right approximately 15 feet. After placing a blue Metolius TCU, she continued up, slotted a nut between a block and the wall, pulled up, and in the process dislodged the entire block, causing her to fall approximately 25 feet. The sharp, heavy block (100 pounds or more) struck her lower left leg. Luckily, her attentive belayer was able to arrest the fall.

MT's shin was bleeding heavily and one of the ropes was cut to the core. She was lowered to the ground and was able to walk unaided the first 2/3 mile to the car. Her partner supported her the last 1/3 mile.

ANALYSIS

According to MT: "We were climbing on half ropes, and four out of the seven core strands and the entire sheath of one rope was cut. The other rope was fine and arrested my fall. As far as I can remember, I was falling at the same speed as the dislodged rock. When the rope finally arrested my fall, I was pulled up into the rock (which is how I got numerous, deep lacerations on my lower left leg and ankle). After the rock crashed past me, I smashed into the rock facing outward, with my butt and upper thigh area sustaining huge bruises and small cuts. My left calf was cut open and ended up swelling twice the size of my right calf.

My advice to other climbers: Learn how to place solid gear and always inspect the quality of the rock. Testing this placement could have prevented my accident. I didn't expect a rock the size of a 1980s microwave to move! (*Source: MT.*)

[*Editor's note: This incident highlights an important benefit of using half (double) ropes, particularly in alpine terrain or crags where loose rock is suspected.*]

FALL ON ROCK | Failure to Test Hold
LINVILLE GORGE, SHORTOFF MOUNTAIN

During the early afternoon of Monday, March 10, Jackson Depew (23) and Zach Patterson (24) were climbing Maginot Line (5.7) on Shortoff Mountain, at the south end of the Linville Gorge Wilderness Area. Jackson was leading the third pitch when he found himself slightly off-route. A hold broke, causing him to fall. Zach was able to control Jackson's fall, but not before he dropped about 35 feet onto a narrow ledge approximately 200 feet up on the route, sustaining multiple injuries that included a concussion, broken leg, fractured pelvis, tailbone, three broken ribs, and a collapsed lung. Because of his condition he was unable to self-rescue. At this time Zach called me (Wesley Calkins) and my climbing partner Dylan Johnston to request assistance.

Because I am intimately acquainted with Shortoff Mountain, I knew exactly where my friends were. When I arrived at the top of Maginot Line, there were three search and rescue personnel on scene. My first interaction with these gentlemen, unfortunately, conformed to every other interaction I have had with them. At their best, they are honorable, well-intentioned volunteers, but they do not spend much time in fifth-class terrain. I asked who was in charge. They didn't know and didn't offer me any plan or directive. Fearing for my friend and unsure what these three gentlemen could possibly do for him, I proceeded to set up a rappel to go down to Jackson. At no time did they direct me not to descend.

I attached my climbing rope to a tree and rappelled approximately 100 feet on a single line with a Grigri. At this point I built a midpoint anchor for the rappel line and continued another 60 feet to Jackson. Dylan also descended the line and positioned himself about 20 feet above.

Jackson was lying in a fetal position. I immediately could tell that he was in a lot of pain. Thanks to my training in technical rescue and wilderness first aid, I began to work. First, I made Jackson safe from falling any farther. I took some gear from his harness and built an anchor about 20 feet above him in a crack system. I secured Jackson to the anchor with his rope. I began assessing and monitoring his condition. I knew that I would not be able to extricate him from the cliff on my own. I knew from his condition that time was a factor and we needed to get him to advanced medical care as quickly as possible. And I knew that the terrain above would not allow for an efficient raising system.

I made cell phone contact with people on top of the cliff and incident command. I gave patient assessments and guided the rescuers where to place their ropes to reach the victim. I tried to be as precise and as helpful as possible.

Poor Zach had been down there belaying for hours. I swapped Jackson's rope out for my own, so that Jackson and I were secured by my rappel line. Then I directed Dylan to bring Zach up on the original climbing rope and get him off the cliff. Plus, I knew that I needed to get off the cliff eventually, so I also told Dylan to be ready to belay me up once the rescuers had taken over. I busied myself with Jackson, knowing that I had a belay no matter what the rescuers did or didn't do.

I made several phone calls to communicate Jackson's progress, so it is difficult to remember when I was first instructed to leave the scene by incident command. However, no one seemed to have a problem when I responded that I would leave the ledge as soon as someone from the rescue squad arrived to care for Jackson. It never occurred to me that they actually wanted me to abandon Jackson without handing him off to a rescuer. I deduced that the incident commander was not on scene, because I could not fathom a directive that instructed me to leave an injured person.

When the first rescuer finally arrived, the rope was too short to reach the victim. It dangled 20 feet above our heads. The rescuer didn't know how to communicate his predicament to the people upstairs. He was doing the best he could, so I carefully directed him on how to use my climbing rope to rappel the remaining distance to reach Jackson. Once I had him on the ledge, he took out a massive first-aid kit, and once I saw him reach down and touch Jackson I didn't feel anything but gratitude, admiration, and relief. Thank God, I thought.

The first thing the rescuer told me was incident command wanted me to leave the scene. Jackson moaned some feeble protests, but I responded by saying that definitive care had arrived and that I needed to let the rescuers take over.

But the rescuer had transferred to my climbing rope during his descent, and

Jackson was still tied to it as well, and both of them were anchored to the crack system 20 feet above their heads. I honestly didn't think the rescuer understood any of this very well. I was reluctant to leave and I wasn't sure how or when he expected me to vacate the ledge. It sounded like more rescuers were on their way, along with a helicopter. It never occurred to me to prusik the line, and the need for my immediate departure was never relayed to me. I told him that I was planning to climb out as soon as they could free up my climbing rope. But they never did. So I simply attached myself to the anchor that was 20 feet away. At the time, it felt like the safest thing for me to do was to wait there.

The helicopter eventually arrived, hovered near the cliff to assess the situation, and then lowered a rescuer with a basket to the ledge.

The two rescuers began packing the victim for extraction. Another paramedic was lowered out of the helicopter and attached the hook to the basket and lifted Jackson away. Then the helicopter lifted away the other two rescuers and I was all alone. I pulled up the now empty rope end, tied in, called up to confirm my belay from Dylan, cleaned all the gear, and climbed with Jackson's rack, my rack, Jackson's pack, and my pack.

When I arrived at the top, I wasn't greeted by rescue personnel, thanked, cared for, or supported. Instead, I was detained by a U.S. Forest Service ranger. He was visibly upset with me and my partner over the situation. I was emotional and more than slightly irritated. The ranger instructed me to hike down the mountain with him. During the two-mile hike, I managed to explain the entire situation that afternoon, and the ranger agreed that something did not sound right—he said that he had been called to the scene to detain a belligerent civilian who was interfering with a professional rescue.

The silent, indifferent eyes of all the rescuers at the trailhead helped me understand what had happened. I believe my actions, my critical thinking, and my decisiveness had embarrassed the search and rescue team members. I had inadvertently robbed them of some pride. The ranger pulled me aside and said, "Look, I admire what you did up there, but I have to do something here, because they are expecting me to arrest you. I'm going to write you a citation for disorderly conduct and you shouldn't worry about it. It's not a criminal citation, it's just a fine. If you pay it, it disappears." Believe it or not, I was grateful. If he had just believed everything the rescuers said, I would have been in jail. As it was, I was free to get in my car and leave, a gesture for which I am immensely grateful.

ANALYSIS

Many times in western North Carolina, you have to run out a pitch—or you may choose to run it out because of your comfort level with the climb. However, any number of things can happen while climbing—including breaking a hold, like in this incident—and protection should be placed conservatively to mitigate the risk of huge falls. (*Source: Wesley Calkins.*)

[*Editor's note: This became a well-publicized and much-discussed incident. We contacted the local first responders for their side of the story but did not receive a response by publication date.*]

FALL ON ROCK, RAPPEL ERROR | Uneven Ropes, No Knots
PISGAH NATIONAL FOREST, LITTLE LOST COVE CLIFFS

During the afternoon of April 12, a male climber (21) fell 70 feet while showing two friends how to rappel. After threading his ropes through the two-bolt anchor at the top of the cliff he began to rappel. Seconds later, his friends stated, the rappeller was out of sight and the rope pulled all the way through the anchor. He was found at the bottom of the cliff with hand and foot fractures, a dislocated shoulder, and head injuries. Rescuers carried the victim half a mile through the woods before reaching an ATV to take him another mile down a narrow trail to a hastily constructed helicopter landing zone. He was flown to Johnson City Medical Center in east Tennessee.

ANALYSIS

Rescuers stated that upon arrival at the scene they found the rope with a friction hitch (type unknown) wrapped around one strand of rope. They also noted that there were no blocking knots tied on the rope ends. It appears the climber failed to equalize the rope ends and misjudged the height of the cliff. He likely rappelled off one end of the rope, causing it to pull through the anchor. A correctly tied rappel backup, incorporating both rope strands, and blocking knots likely would have prevented this incident. (*Source: Corey Winstead, Appalachian Mountain Rescue.*)

FALL ON ROCK | No Anchor, Poor Position
STONE MOUNTAIN STATE PARK

Late in the afternoon on Saturday, June 7, Lisa Bacon (31) and Brian Sakofsky (35) fell approximately 60 feet from the Tree Ledge while rappelling the south face of Stone Mountain. Both sustained life-threatening injuries. Bacon was taken by an Air Care

helicopter to Wake Forest Baptist Hospital, in Winston-Salem, while Sakofsky was taken by ground.

ANALYSIS

Park officials, along with members of the Carolina Climbers Coalition, conducted an investigation to determine the cause of the accident. This involved examination of the accident scene and inspection of equipment. The climbers were not interviewed.

Lisa's harness was attached to the climbing rope by a locking carabiner through the belay/rappel loop and a partially finished figure 8 knot tied to that carabiner. The rope had been cut a few feet above the knot, apparently by

[Left] Two climbers were probably preparing to lower from this tree when they fell to the ground at Stone Mountain. *Brian Payst*

ESSENTIALS
RAPPELLING

BY NATHAN OLLSON

In 2012 we published a Know the Ropes article by UIAGM/IFMGA guide Rob Hess about the causes and prevention of rappelling accidents. Since rappel errors continue to cause many accidents, we offer these essential reminders.

The three leading causes of rappel incidents reported in *Accidents* are:

1. Inadequate anchor systems/anchor failure (26%).
2. Inadequate backups (19%).
3. Rappelling off the end of the rope(s), largely due to uneven rope ends (29%).

These accidents can be mitigated through the following practices:

[Above] This image shows extension of a rappel device using a personal anchor system, or PAS. (This can also be accomplished with a nylon sling.) A friction hitch is in place on the brake-hand side of the rope as a backup. Extension gives the climber more control over a rappel. The free end of the PAS can be clipped into anchors during multi-pitch descents. *Rick Weber*

ANCHORING SYSTEMS

Anchor failure may be the result of worn equipment, the climber carrying inadequate equipment for building an anchor, or having inadequate opportunities to build an anchor. To prevent such accidents:

• Inspect personal gear, fixed anchors, and rock quality. In particular, look for wear on slings or rappel rings, loose bolts, or aging pitons or other fixed gear. In the alpine environment, areas with melt/freeze cycles, or places with soft/poor rock, these checks are imperative. Don't hesitate to back up suspicious anchors.
• On multi-pitch routes, carry anchor-building equipment including double-length slings, cordelette or extra webbing, quick links/extra carabiners/rappel rings, and a small knife to remove worn webbing.
• Build anchors with equalized and redundant components.

RAPPEL SYSTEMS AND BACKUPS

Tangled ropes and other issues can be avoided with a good rappel system that includes a backup. Such a system has:

• A rappel device extended away from the climber   **[CONTINUED NEXT PAGE...]**

with a nylon sling or personal anchor system (PAS).

• A friction hitch such as an auto-block tied on the brake-hand side of the rappel system, clipped to the harness belay loop, and shortened to avoid contact with the belay device.

• A "fireman's belay": after the first climber rappels, he or she can hold the rope ends and pull them tight if the next climber loses control.

• A nylon sling or PAS girth-hitched through the tie-in point(s) of the harness for clipping to anchors. Daisy chains and long lengths of Dyneema should not to be used as personal anchoring slings.

ROPE MANAGEMENT

To avoid rappelling off the ends of unknotted and/or uneven ropes, rig the ropes properly before a rappel:

• Study descriptions of the descent route before any climb and carry a topo.

• Be aware of rope length(s) and middle marks.

• Knot the individual rope ends, except in situations where they may become jammed or tangled. In such conditions carry the rope ends "saddlebag style" in stacked coils, cradled in slings and clipped to the harness' gear or leg loops.

• When joining two ropes, use a well-dressed flat overhand knot, including tails of 12 inches or longer.

• Be prepared to ascend the rope. Know how to improvise friction hitches and/or carry ascending devices.

• Use gloves for more control over the rappel speed.

Search "Know the Ropes: Rappelling" online to find the complete 2012 article.

rescue personnel. This configuration suggests the climber was not tied into the rope while moving around on the Tree Ledge before attaching it to the locking carabiner. Her harness also had a belay/rappel device and a nut tool attached to the gear loops. Because the rappel device was not attached to the rope or in a position to be used, it is unlikely she was preparing to rappel at the time she fell. There were no slings or carabiners attached to her harness that would indicate that she was clipped in or able to be clipped in to a fixed anchor.

Brian's harness was severely abraded on the leg and waist loops, most likely from sliding down the lower angle rock below the Tree Ledge. There was a personal anchor system (PAS) girth-hitched through the belay/rappel loop, a very typical set-up for clipping into anchors. The rope was not attached to Brian's harness. An additional 48-inch sling was doubled over into a 24-inch length and clipped to the PAS with two locking carabiners. The absence of a carabiner on the end of the 48-inch sling or the PAS suggests the climber was not clipped into an anchor at the time of the fall, nor was he immediately ready to do so. One possible scenario is that Brian intended to wrap the 48-inch sling around a tree or rock and use that as anchor, but the sling likely would not have reached around the tree closest to where the fall occurred.

The top of the Entrance Crack, at the right end of Tree Ledge, was the most likely location from where the climbers fell (based on where they landed and what information the rangers had). There were no signs of an anchor on the tree at the top of the Entrance Crack, nor in the surrounding area, indicating the climbers were not secured at the time of the accident. A two-bolt anchor is located approximately 15 feet above and climber's left of this tree, but no gear was found attached to it.

Based on the investigation, both Brian and Lisa were likely preparing to rappel or lower from the large tree located at the top of the Entrance Crack. Brian has stated that Lisa was going "over the tree" when she slipped and fell down the face, and he fell while trying to grab her. If this is accurate, this suggests that Brian likely was going to use the tree to assist in lowering Lisa, who was apparently anxious to be on the ground. Lowering a climber is fairly standard practice, however typically the rope would be passed around the tree and secured to the climber being lowered while both climbers were safely anchored to the cliff. Neither climber appears to have been anchored.

The Grigri found with Brian's equipment was closed and attached to a locking carabiner, but not the rope, suggesting that Lisa was not on belay while moving around the tree. It is likely that Brian was preparing to put Lisa on belay when the accident occurred.

The two-bolt anchor near the accident scene is located on a small, flat ledge and is easily accessible—it is one of the primary means of descent from the Tree Ledge. The anchor location is not easily visible from above, due to the angle of the rock, but is visible when looking back up the cliff from the tree. The climbers' 70-meter rope would have reached the ground from these bolted anchors. The climbers appear to have been unfamiliar with the area and the descent options.

In conclusion, this was an avoidable accident, with safer descent options being readily available. Most likely a combination of anxiety and a lack of appropriate edge awareness resulted in Lisa losing her balance and falling down the face. If Brian tried to grab her from his position at the top of Entrance Crack, it is easy to see how he could have lost his balance or been pulled off by her weight. (*Source: Edited from a report by Brian Payst, Carolina Climbers Coalition.*)

FALL ON ROCK, RAPPEL ERROR | Uneven Ropes, No Knots
CROWDERS MOUNTAIN STATE PARK, PRACTICE WALL

During the early afternoon on September 1, Ben Lee (28) fell while rappelling Burn Crack (5.10c) on the Practice Wall. He was on rappel with an ATC when one of the ropes on the double-rope rappel pulled through the device, causing him to fall 15 to 20 feet to the ground. He was placed in a Stokes basket and carried to a waiting ambulance, which transported him to the hospital where he underwent surgery. (*Source: Crowders Mountain State Park.*)

ANALYSIS

In this incident knots on both ends of the rope would have resulted in a different outcome. Before descending, always do a pre-rappel check: You and your partner(s) should check the anchor, check the ropes to be sure they reach their intended destination and are even, and be sure they have blocking knots on both ends. Check the rappel device to make sure that it is set up and oriented correctly, check the carabiner gate (locked), and assess the need for a backup. (*Source: Aram Attarian.*)

OREGON

FALL ON SNOW | Cornice Collapse, Climbing Unroped, Poor Position
MT. HOOD, SOUTH SIDE

On May 13, Robert Cormier (57) attempted to summit Mt. Hood via the popular South Side Route with two companions. One team member suffered a leg cramp, and the party separated as Cormier summited ahead of his companions. He traversed too far north from the summit rim and caused a cornice collapse. This resulted in a 700-foot fall over very steep terrain onto the upper Eliot Glacier, causing fatal injuries.

ANALYSIS

Corniced summits and ridges are often deceptive, as the cornices usually cannot be seen when approaching from the windward side. When in doubt, a climbing party should protect themselves with a belay. When cornicing is suspected or visible, staying well below the crest of the cornice may prevent it from fracturing. Warm air temperatures can increase the hazard by weakening the snow and ice. (*Source: Jeff Scheetz, Portland Mountain Rescue.*)

FALL ON SNOW/ICE | Failure to Self-Arrest
MT. HOOD, SOUTH SIDE

On May 24, James Adams (59) slipped on ice while descending the South Side Route. He was unable to self-arrest and slid several hundred feet into a fumarole (an opening in a glacier caused by ice melting due to volcanic fumes). Others witnessed his fall and communicated with a nearby Portland Mountain Rescue team. After verbal contact was made with the subject, a rescuer was lowered 100 feet into the fumarole and performed a medical assessment of Adams. After he was stabilized, Adams was raised to the surface and evacuated via helicopter to Legacy Emanuel Medical Center. He

[Below] Rescuers work to retrieve a climber who slid into a fumarole on Mt. Hood. Fumaroles are volcanic gas vents that melt crevasse-like openings into the ice. These gases can be toxic, and climbers and rescuers must avoid inhaling them. *Scott Norton / Portland Mountain Rescue*

suffered multiple fractures, abrasions, and contusions but did survive. (*Source: Jeff Scheetz, Portland Mountain Rescue.*)

FALL ON SNOW | Exceeding Abilities, Weather
MIDDLE SISTER

On November 12, Ryan Burton (25) and Benjamin Newkirk (39) left the trailhead at Pole Creek and hiked six miles to Camp Lake, where they set camp and rested before departing around 6:30 p.m. Weather reports at the time and for the three days following the incident included warnings for high wind and large amounts of snow. The party was aware of the forecasts and expected the weather to arrive at around 10 p.m. that night. The party wanted to summit before the storm hit and believed they had the ability and equipment to survive the storm if they were caught.

The two men climbed the southeast ridge (Grade II, 4th class) and reached the 10,056-foot summit at around 9:42 p.m. They began their descent at around 10 p.m., after resting, eating, and drinking water on top. Weather conditions around this time included temperatures of about -5°C (23°F), wind of 20 mph, and visibility of about 30 feet. The party was unroped. At around 9,600 feet, Newkirk experienced a fatal fall; at the time, he was out of sight of Burton and about 30 feet upslope. Burton recalled that Newkirk slid past him with his feet downhill, on his back, and with a functioning headlamp, making no visible attempt to arrest his fall. He was wearing a helmet, a backpack, and crampons. Burton's visual and verbal searches returned no indication of Newkirk. Burton called his father and then 911, and then descended to Camp Lake. He was evacuated the following day. Newkirk was located on November 16 and was extracted via helicopter.

ANALYSIS

The weather on a high peak in winter is not to be underestimated. The knowledge of an impending storm most likely hastened the party's descent and partially contributed to the fall. Even if the subject's injuries were survivable, rescue would have been impossible due to the storm. On this particular route, climbing unroped is generally considered to be reasonable and expected. (*Source: Matt Crawford, Deschutes County Search and Rescue.*)

[*Editor's note: According to an article in The Bulletin, an Oregon newspaper, Burton told officials after the accident that Newkirk had indicated he was "bonking" high on the mountain, and Burton believed Newkirk was already unconscious when he fell, explaining why he apparently made no attempt to self-arrest.*]

FALL ON SNOW | Ski Mountaineering
MT. JEFFERSON

Around 4:30 or 5 p.m. on July 21, after skiing down the Whitewater Glacier high on Mt. Jefferson, Miko Smilenski lost an edge during a steep turn and fell about 100 feet near treeline. The 56-year-old experienced skier hit many exposed rocks during the slide and suffered a broken femur and head trauma. After activating his personal locator beacon (PLB), the well-equipped ski mountaineer was able to shelter himself, surviving the night until a Blackhawk helicopter evacuation the next morning.

ANALYSIS

Solo mountaineering and skiing have inherent risks that some choose to accept. In this case, experience and equipment were instrumental in the survival of the subject. He was carrying a plastic bivouac sack and an inflatable sleeping pad that protected him from the snow overnight. It is not known if ski pole self-arresting devices were used. (*Source: Jeff Scheetz, Portland Mountain Rescue.*)

FALL ON ROCK | Exceeding Abilities, Inadequate Protection
SMITH ROCK STATE PARK, ZEBRA ZION

On May 4, Forrest Koran (24) and Suruthai Pokaratsiri-Goldstein (27) began climbing a four-pitch trad route called Zebra Zion (5.10a). The climbers were members of an "Advanced Rock" class hosted by a local climbing organization. Koran led the fourth and final pitch, placing two small cams before he fell with about 15 feet of rope between himself and the belayer. Both cams pulled out and Koran impacted a 70–80° slab of rock after falling about 30 feet. He was reported to be unconscious for several minutes after the fall. (He was wearing a helmet.) The belayer tied off the belay at the anchor, called 911, and waited for rescue. Rescuers reached the climbers from above, and Koran was lowered approximately 500 feet and taken by helicopter to the hospital, where he was diagnosed with a sprained ankle, minor concussion, and minor injuries.

ANALYSIS

The injured climber was moderately experienced, with more time in the gym than outdoors, and he was leading a four-pitch 5.10 route that was likely beyond his abilities. His mentor was reportedly a 5.11 climber, but not a certified guide. Both cams placed by the subject failed to hold the fall—one cam's lobes were folded inside-out in a manner consistent with a cam placement that is too small for the crack. Fall factors are greatest closest to the belayer, and therefore it is advisable to place more pieces in the first 15 to 30 feet of a pitch, especially in locations with consequential terrain below (in this case the slab under the belay). No effort was made to self-rescue. (*Source: Matt Crawford, Deschutes County Search and Rescue.*)

[Above] This climber fell from the start of the fourth pitch of Zebra Zion at Smith Rock and awaits help from rescuers. Both of the cams the climber had placed for protection failed to hold when he fell. *Vaqas Malik*

FALL ON ROCK | Protection Pulled Out
SMITH ROCK STATE PARK, CHOUINARD'S CRACK

On October 19, Ted Wogan (22) and Climber 2 began climbing Chouinard's Crack (5.9) late in the afternoon. Wogan placed one piece of protection and followed it with a second piece at 25 feet. He initially placed a cam but then, wanting to save the cam for later, replaced it with a hex. At around 30 feet, Wogan fell but was held by the hex. He did not inspect the hex as he climbed past it a second time, and when he fell again at 30 feet the piece failed to hold his fall. He believes that some of his fall was held by the rope, indicating the belay was as effective as possible. He fell to the ground and onto his back and suffered spinal fractures, rib fractures, a scapula fracture, lacerations, and pulmonary contusions. He was released after a three-day hospital stay.

ANALYSIS

It is generally beneficial to place numerous pieces in the first 15–30 feet of a pitch or above a ledge. Additionally, it is important to inspect gear after falling on it to ensure that it is still placed securely. It's not known if Wogan extended the hex with a quickdraw or sling, which may help prevent a piece from being pulled out of position by the action of the rope. (*Source: Matt Crawford, Deschutes County Search and Rescue.*)

[*Editor's note: Another climber fell off Chouinard's Crack earlier in 2014 and hit a ledge, injuring his ankle.*]

SOUTH DAKOTA

FALL ON ROCK | Inadequate Belay
VICTORIA CANYON, FOOT FIST WAY

Jimmy Burckhard, 31, was climbing the bolted route Foot Fist Way (5.13a) in a limestone canyon southwest of Rapid City on September 26. He had previously worked on the route a couple of weeks earlier. On this day he climbed partway up the route, yelled "take," and his belayer held him for a rest. He continued up the climb and then, at about 70 feet, near the top of the route, he let go again. He expected to take a short fall, then lower and rest to attempt the redpoint. Instead he plunged toward the ground, impacting on his heels. Burckhard broke both feet, his wrist and thumb, and three vertebrae in his back.

A local climber hiked out of the canyon to a point where he could get cell reception and dialed 911. Responders carried Burckhard out of the canyon to an ambulance.

ANALYSIS

Burckhard was climbing with one of his regular partners, and both men are very experienced climbers. The belayer was using an assisted-braking device, and when Burckhard asked him after the accident what had happened, he responded, "The device failed." No further information was available. (*Source: The Editors.*)

TENNESSEE

FALL ON ROCK | Inadequate Protection
TENNESSEE WALL, AIN'T SO EAZY

My friends and I decided to end a day of climbing in late February with a 5.9 arête called Ain't So Eazy. No one in our group had tried it before. Before starting the climb I expressed some concerns to my belayer: The bottom holds were wet, the climb looked like it wandered a lot, and it didn't appear to protect well. Regardless, I pulled on and started climbing. I have little recollection of climbing the route but remember expressing concern about the lack of quality pro. My last vague memory is pausing to place a 0.1 Camalot X4 (the smallest size in the X4 range) in a shallow, horizontal slot. I couldn't get the piece to set properly and was starting to feel fatigued, so I left it and moved on. Shortly afterward I hit a crux on the climb and fell. The tiny cam popped out. It was placed approximately 10 to 15 feet above a nut.

I was about 40 to 50 feet above the 12-foot-high boulder at the start of the route. The less-than-vertical nature of the climb, combined with some benefit from the cam before it popped out, probably slowed my fall. After tumbling down the rock, I hit the pointed boulder at the base and started to slide down its side. I regained consciousness as my friends guided me down to the ground. I was in shock and my adrenaline kicked in. I relentlessly tried to convince my friends to "pick me up and go." I wanted to flee the scene. My friends resisted my pleas and held me down for nearly three hours while we waited for rescuers to arrive.

Several climbers nearby, along with two of my friends, were medical workers or certified Wilderness First Responders. I'm grateful that these knowledgeable people were there to help. It was imperative that I was kept still. Later, the neurosurgeon said I nearly had been paralyzed due to shattered vertebrae pushing up against my spinal cord. My friends keeping me still may have prevented my spinal cord from being severed.

The Chattanooga–Hamilton County Cave/ Cliff Rescue team arrived around 9 p.m. and wheeled me down the mountain in a litter, creating belay systems using the trees. An ambulance drove me a short distance to a helicopter pad, and then I was airlifted to Erlanger Hospital. The diagnosis was a fractured skull, four shattered or fractured vertebrae (T11, T12, L1, L2), several broken ribs, a brain bleed, and mild hypothermia.

ANALYSIS

I think my main mistake was choosing a climb with inadequate protection. However, there are other factors to be taken into consideration. (1) I forgot to put on my helmet, which I almost always wear while trad climbing. The severity of my head injury may have been drastically reduced if I had been wearing a helmet. (2) I didn't use good judgment. This climb followed an arête, and I knew that many arêtes at T-Wall don't protect well. In addition, I had expressed a variety of concerns about the climb to my belayer before pulling onto the climb. From this point on, I will fully assess whether the risks are appropriate before starting a route.

This incident has inspired me to get certified as a Wilderness First Responder. It also demonstrates how important it is to have partners who know what to do in these types of situations. (*Source: Brittany Decker.*)

ESSENTIALS

HEAD INJURIES

BY R. BRYAN SIMON

Traumatic brain injury (TBI) is caused by the exertion of a sudden force on the head and brain that causes an abrupt back and forth motion. An impact of this nature can fracture the skull, bruise the brain, tear blood vessels, and destroy neurons. Climbers should be ready to recognize and address a potential head injury after any blow to the head from a climbing fall or from falling rocks, ice, or other objects.

IDENTIFICATION & ASSESSMENT

Quick identification of a head injury is important for reducing long-term harm or preventing mortality to an injured climber. Often these head injuries are associated with other life-threatening conditions, so rescuers also must be prepared to address airway, breathing, circulation, and possible injury to the cervical spine. Immediate medical care should be sought for any climber with TBI.

A climber's level of consciousness is an important proxy for underlying brain damage, and can be rapidly assessed using the mnemonic **AVPU**. This is useful information to convey to rescuers or medical personnel before they arrive on scene.

A – Awake (alert and oriented to person, place, time, and event)
V – Responds to verbal stimuli (awakens, withdraws, or moans when spoken to)
P – Responds to painful stimuli (awakens, withdraws, or moans in response to pain)
U – Unresponsive (no response to any stimuli)

Common signs and symptoms of head injury include:

• Increasing headache
• Change in level of consciousness (increasing sleepiness, confusion or combativeness, or anyone with any persistent finding other than "A" on AVPU scale)
• Difficulty with vision
• Raccoon eyes (bruising around the eyes)
• Battle's sign (bruising behind the ears)
• Persistent and/or projectile vomiting
• Urinary or bowel incontinence

[CONTINUED NEXT PAGE...]

• Bleeding and/or clear drainage from ears or nose
• Seizures
• Weakness or numbness in any part of the body
• One pupil significantly larger than the other

TREATMENT

If any of the signs and symptoms listed above are present, immediate evacuation is essential. Call 911, Global Rescue, or the local rescue dispatch as soon as possible. The time to evacuation of a climber with a head injury directly correlates with survivability and better outcomes. If TBI is suspected and rapid evacuation is not available, the following actions are recommended:

• If the patient is hanging from a rope or stranded high on a route, lower him or her to the ground or a ledge. The risks of damage to the spine or internal injuries must be balanced with the need to get the patient out of immediate danger.
• In sloping terrain, keep the patient's head uphill.
• Monitor the patient's airway and breathing; watch for changes in rate and character.
• Be prepared to "log roll" the patient to one side if he or she vomits. Maintain cervical spine; i.e., immobilize head, neck, and back, and move the body as a unit.
• Wake the victim every 3 to 4 hours to monitor condition and changes in consciousness.

References: *Field Guide to Wilderness Medicine* (4th edition), by Auerbach, Constance, and Freer, 2013. "Wilderness Trauma and Surgical Emergencies," by Gross, Collier, Riordan, et al, included in *Wilderness Medicine* (6th edition), 2012.

R. Bryan Simon, a registered nurse and co-owner of Vertical Medicine Resources, is the climbing medicine columnist for the magazine Wilderness Medicine.

UTAH

ROCKFALL | Late Start, Darkness

MT. OLYMPUS, WEST SLABS

On July 5, Mary Ann Overfelt and I set out to tackle the West Slabs of Mt. Olympus (1,600', 5.5), east of Salt Lake City. We started hiking a bit later than we would have liked, but still reached the start of the route about 11 a.m. A few other parties were in the vicinity, but we felt we could move at a good pace and that daylight would not be an issue. The West Slabs are very wide and low-angle, with dozens of variations. I am a very experienced climber (12-plus years), but this was Mary Ann's second time climbing. That said, she is a quick study and easily tackled this challenge.

By the time we reached the large ledge near the top it was 1.5 to 2 hours before sunset. We spent a bit of time on the ledge and considered our options before deciding to rappel the gully to the west via a number of fixed slings on trees. After three rappels we reached a point where we could begin to scramble. Wisely, we kept our helmets on. The scramble was loose, dirty, and sometimes rather steep. As darkness fell in the canyon we continued our descent but did not feel the need to turn on our headlamps; we could see the way quite easily.

About two-thirds of the way down the main scrambling section, Mary Ann noticed something large hurtling down the cliff toward us. She immediately yelled, "Rock, rock, rock!" Instinctively, we both dropped and tried to make smaller targets. I was carrying the larger pack and had the rope strapped to my pack (and a helmet on), and by going into "turtle mode" I was well-protected. Mary Ann was able to press herself against the lower wall.

The large rock broke into a number of smaller chunks. Several small to medium-size rocks hit Mary Ann's helmet, leg, and hip; she sustained some bruising and abrasions. Numerous small pieces rained down on me, striking my helmet and pack, but did not cause any injuries. A few larger pieces bounced around us.

As we continued down, we looked up and noticed two headlamps high above us on the big ledge. We concluded that the climbing party likely had dislodged the rock that came down at us. Given the distance, it would have been difficult for us to hear them clearly yelling "rock!" We completed the rest of the two-mile scramble and hike back to the car without incident.

ANALYSIS

Mary Ann was exceptionally quick to recognize the large rock coming toward us, immediately yell "rock!" and get herself into the safest position possible. Again, this was her second time climbing.

Had we started earlier and descended with more daylight, we might have seen the rock falling sooner and avoided any impacts. Perhaps the most important thing is that both of us were still wearing our helmets. Many climbers choose to (A) not wear helmets (dumb) or (B) take them off when descending (nearly as dumb as A). Keeping our helmets on might well have saved our lives. (*Source: Andrew Weinmann.*)

[*Editor's note: It's equally important to consider donning your helmet during an approach. Many climbers don't put on a helmet until they reach the base of a route and start gearing up. It should go on as soon as you reach terrain exposed to potential rockfall or icefall, whether natural or climber-caused.*]

FALL ON ROCK | Inadequate Protection
BELL'S CANYON, BELL'S BEAST

On November 7, Michael Lydon (50) was killed after falling down nearly a full pitch of moderate terrain at the top of Beast (5.11a), a five-pitch climb on the Bell's Beast formation. Lydon and his partner, Chris Wood (33), had first climbed Beauty (5.11b), then rappelled to a ledge below pitch two of Beast. Chris led and linked the second and third pitches of Beast, which Mike followed. Chris led the fourth pitch, and when Mike got to the anchor he decided he'd keep climbing to the anchors at the top of the 5.5 final pitch. Near the top of the fifth pitch, Mike fell due to an unknown cause. At this point he had not placed any protection since leaving the anchor. He fell past the belay and impacted the slab below.

Chris secured the belay and rappelled to Mike. He began first aid and called 911. Resources from the Salt Lake County Search and Rescue team and Unified Fire Authority were immediately mobilized. Rescuers utilized an Intermountain Life Flight helicopter to access the ridgeline above the climb. When the rescuer reached the climbing party, he determined that Mike had expired from his injuries. The decision was made to lower the rescuer and Chris to safety and recover Mike's body the following day.

ANALYSIS

Both of these climbs are protected with a mix of bolts and removable protection, and climbers normally carry a rack of cams and nuts in addition to quickdraws. The deceased was a highly experienced climber and chose to run it out on easy, although loose, ground. Placing even a single good piece to prevent a fall onto a ledge or lower angle terrain might have saved his life. (*Source: Justin Grisham and Ben Robertson, Salt Lake County SAR.*)

FALL ON ROCK

INDIAN CREEK, SUPERCRACK BUTTRESS

On the day before Thanksgiving, a 24-year-old climber was top-roping her last climb of the day: Gorilla (5.10). Approximately 15 feet up the climb, her foot slipped out of a jam while her left hand was jammed in the crack. As she fell her hand stayed stuck in the crack too long, and she suffered a hairline fracture of her radius. Our group splinted the arm and drove her to the hospital in Moab, where she was diagnosed and treated. She climbed using just her right arm the next day!

ANALYSIS

The climber hadn't checked her foot before weighting it, and the jam was pretty insecure. In crack climbing, as in all styles of climbing, good footwork is the most important element of success. (*Source: Chris S.*)

[Left] The splitter jams of Gorilla at Supercrack Buttress, Utah. *Mike McLaughlin*

RAPPEL ERROR | Possible Equipment Failure

ARCHES NATIONAL PARK, TOWER OF BABEL

On September 23 a climber fell between 75 and 100 feet while rappelling Zenyatta Entrada (5.4 C3) on the Tower of Babel. NPS rangers responded to the scene and found the climber lying on the ground at the base of the route. His partner was still descending from the second pitch. The victim was evacuated by wheeled litter to the road and taken by helicopter to a trauma center in Grand Junction, Colorado.

The fallen climber and his partner had ascended the route and were rappelling when the accident occurred. The first climber, leading the rappels, was out of sight of his partner. The partner above said the ropes began to pull rapidly through the anchor. He tried to grab the rope, but it was moving too fast and burned his hands. Later, the fallen climber stated that he had fallen off the end of the rope. However, at the base of the climb rescuers found a broken carabiner that had connected the climber's ATC rappel device to his harness. The partner stated that the victim had been having problems with that carabiner throughout the day.

According to an online forum post by the partner, the climber had eight broken ribs, several broken fingers, and a collapsed lung, but was expected to make a full recovery. He was wearing a helmet. (*Source: Arches National Park/NPS Emergency Services.*)

ANALYSIS

The climbers were using two ropes to rappel, but it's unclear whether the ropes had reached the ground. Based on the broken carabiner discovered at the base, it would seem this accident could be attributed to equipment failure or misuse rather than rappelling off the end of the ropes (though that is still possible). An open-gate or nose-hooked carabiner could have resulted in a break that caused the victim to become detached from the ropes. (*Source: The Editors.*)

FALL ON ROCK | Protection Pulled Out, Rockfall
GLEN CANYON RECREATION AREA, LAKE POWELL

On April 5, a 30-year-old male climber from Grand Junction, Colorado, began aid-soloing up Gregory Butte, located near the mouth of Last Chance Bay, at 7 a.m. A little after 9 a.m., he was over 500 feet up the wall when a piece he had placed pulled out, causing him to fall approximately 30 feet. His fall was stopped by lower gear placements, but when the first piece failed it also caused a large slab of stone to break free. This fell and hit the climber in the head, severely injuring him.

The climber had completed several shorter climbs on Gregory Butte during the two previous days, and several of his friends were watching him from a boat. They drove to an area where they could get cell phone coverage, and they notified rescue personnel, who responded by boat and helicopter to the scene. The helicopter transported three Kane County SAR personnel and gear from Kanab, Utah, to the top of Gregory Butte, where they joined with the Glen Canyon SAR team. Five rescuers drilled and set anchors on top of the Butte, and a medic was lowered to the injured climber. He was able to secure the climber, and both were raised back to the top by the other four rescuers.

The injured climber was flown to a hospital in Flagstaff, Arizona. His injuries were serious, but he was expected to recover. He was wearing a helmet at the time of the accident, and rescuers attribute it with saving his life. (*Source: Kane County Emergency Services.*)

FALL ON ROCK | Climbing Unroped
ZION NATIONAL PARK, SPEARHEAD

On October 19, Christopher Spencer (47) of San Jose, California, was killed after falling from the approach to Iron Messiah (5.10+) on the Spearhead formation. Spencer and his partner were scrambling up the easy (low 5th class) but exposed buttress to the base of the technical pitches, when Spencer slipped and fell about 80 feet, hitting several ledges during the fall. He was not roped in or wearing a helmet.

Rangers responded to reports of the incident about 11 a.m. and reached Spencer and his climbing partner by noon. He was airlifted out, and medics were able to stabilize him during the rescue effort, which took nearly three hours, but Spencer died of his injuries at a hospital in St. George, Utah, later that day. (*Source: Zion National Park.*)

ANALYSIS

Iron Messiah is generally climbed in eight or nine pitches, with a long rappel descent. Eager to start a big day of climbing, many climbers choose to scramble the approach up a bushy ramp system to reach the first "real" pitch. This approach of a couple of hundred feet is 4th class or low 5th class, depending on the exact route followed. Given the exposure and Zion's somewhat loose, sandy rock, great care obviously is needed. Simul-climbing is an alternative to soloing or belayed climbing on such approaches, but there is potential to snag the rope or pull off loose rocks. Consider shortening the rope for simul-climbing. As noted in the Mt. Olympus incident above, helmets should be worn during a technical approach as well as the climb, especially on a popular route when other climbers may be overhead. (*Source: The Editors.*)

FALL ON ROCK | Inadequate Protection, Top-Roping Error
ZION NATIONAL PARK, KOLOB CANYON

On April 6 a female climber (approximately 20 years old) broke her leg after taking a large, swinging top-rope fall from a sport climb in Kolob Canyon. The climber was part of a group of seven that visited the very overhanging crag that day. The group had one lead climber, who hung draws and left top-ropes on the two easiest routes at the crag: a 5.10+ and 5.11-. None of the other climbers in the group was able to complete these routes on top-rope, and each climber cleaned the quickdraws to his or her respective high point, leaving fewer directionals for each subsequent climber. At some point each climber swung away from the wall and was unable to regain it.

The lead climber cleaned these two routes, then led a wildly overhanging 5.12a, resting at each bolt. On his way down, he cleaned all of the quickdraws, leaving the

[Right] The severely overhanging climbs of Kolob Canyon require directionals for safe top-roping. *Courtesy of Ben Iseman*

rope hanging directly from the anchors to the ground, about 40 to 50 feet from the base of the wall. The victim then began climbing the 12a on top-rope with no quickdraws in place as directionals. She climbed to the first bolt, asked for her belayer to take, and fell. She swung about 40 feet out from the wall and impacted a rock, breaking her left leg. Another party at the crag made sure the group had adequate insulation, water and headlamps, and hiked out to notify park officials. Rescuers responded and the victim was evacuated from the canyon that night.

ANALYSIS

The victim's uncontrolled swing could have been prevented by leaving some quickdraws in as directional anchors. The draws were removed because the lead climber doubted that any of his friends would be able to complete the route. The injured climber later told the others that she knew it was a bad idea to climb the route without directionals, but had deferred to her more experienced friend.

Other contributing factors include a large group of inexperienced climbers at a remote, backcountry crag, top-roping through worn fixed anchors in soft sandstone, and lack of first-aid training. [*Source: Ben Iseman, witnessing party.*]

VERMONT

FALL ON ICE | Ascending Error, Darkness

MT. PISGAH (LAKE WILLOUGHBY), THE TABLETS

On December 27, 2013, at the base of the center Tablet at Lake Willoughby, my friend John (37) and I (32) congratulated ourselves after a 60-meter rappel to the ground, shortly after sunset. We had just finished our third two-pitch ice route that day—one route on each of the Tablets. It was our seventh day of ice climbing for the season, only our second winter of ice climbing. I had three years of trad climbing experience and a good working knowledge of rope systems and self-rescue. John was one of my primary climbing partners over the past year; he had come to climbing only two years earlier. He lacked much of the climbing experience I had, though he took a course in crevasse rescue in preparation for a Mt. Rainier climb we had done together the previous spring. He was also an avid reader of climbing books.

I went to pull the rappel ropes and found they would not budge. I confirmed with John that I was pulling on the correct rope. We decided to pull together, hoping to overcome the unknown obstacle, but it was to no avail. I decided to pull on the other end of the rope and found that it slid with little effort for about a foot and then stopped. The ropes would not move any farther in either direction.

I thought back to how I had threaded our ropes at the top before rappelling. We had rappelled off a tree that had two or three loops of tubular webbing tied around the base and no rappel rings. Being thrifty and not wanting to leave a carabineer, I had taken one rope and threaded it from bottom to top between the tree and webbing. I then tied our ropes together with an overhand knot, leaving two=foot-long tails. On one of the tails I tied a backup knot so the primary overhand knot would not roll over itself. With this setup, we would be pulling the rope up and over the webbing around the

[Above] The two-pitch left and center Tablet routes at Lake Willoughby. A climber fell 20 to 25 feet down the right-hand flow while trying to retrieve stuck rappel ropes. *John Albers*

tree. However, our pulling apparently had cinched the webbing tighter around the trunk and was pinching the rope with sufficient force to prevent it from being pulled through.

One of us had to ascend the rappel lines and fix the jam, and I began setting up for this. Knowing that John had voiced a desire to assume more responsibility with our rappels, I offered the job to him, which he reluctantly took. As I was tying the knots and preparing the system, I hastily explained what I was doing and how the system would work. In retrospect, I recall thinking it was odd that John was listening to me as if he had not ascended a rope before. He had taken a crevasse rescue class, after all.

John headed up the rope, reaching a large ledge about 15 to 20 feet up, and then walked across this before starting up the remaining 150 feet or so. I had occupied myself with some trail mix and hot water and was not paying much attention at this point. However, it was clear to me that he was becoming frustrated, as he began shouting down that it was going to take too long to climb the rope. He suggested we leave the rope overnight and deal with it in the morning.

About 20 to 25 feet above the large ledge, he came to a rocky overhang. He felt it would be easier to go around the overhang instead of passing over it. He held on to the rope and was reaching out with his crampon and beginning to pull himself over when he suddenly began to fall. I heard a scream and looked up to see a headlamp tumbling in the dark and landing on the ledge out of my sight. I grabbed my ice tools and began climbing up to the ledge, shouting to John, "Don't move!" I was relieved to hear him shout back, "I am OK, I am OK."

At the ledge, John was standing and reported that he was not experiencing any pain. He did not know why he fell. However, he recalled that when he fell he was holding on to the rappel lines and that he held onto them all the way to the ledge.

ANALYSIS

A number of factors were at play. First the ropes were improperly set up for a clean pull after the rappel. This easily could have been prevented if we had checked to make sure they slid smoothly before rappelling to the bottom. [*Editor's note: Attaching carabiners or rappel rings to the webbing and threading the rope through them is a better way to ensure a smooth pull and protect the webbing.*]

Second, we were not completely aware of each other's skill levels. At John's crevasse rescue course, apparently they had only talked about ascending a rope and did not do any hands-on practice. Had I known this, I would not have suggested that he ascend the ropes and fix the rappel. Third, John was frustrated by the delay and was not mentally focused on the task at hand.

Fourth, when John began to fall he was grabbing the ropes above both prusiks. This pushed the prusiks down the rope with him as he fell and prevented them from being weighted and potentially stopping his fall.

Finally, John had not tied back up knots in the rope that would have prevented him from falling all the way to the ledge. (*Source: Chris.*)

[*Editor's note: Backup knots could have caused problems when rappelling back down the ropes after they were freed, especially in the dark. A better safeguard when ascending icy rappel ropes is to use a metal/mechanical ascender, such as a Tibloc, in place of one prusik hitch. These also are less vulnerable to slipping if a climber inadvertently grabs the rope. This 2013 incident did not make it into Accidents 2014, and we've published it here for its instructional value. It is not included in our 2014 tables.*]

VIRGINIA

FALL ON ROCK | Inadequate Belay, Inexperience

RICHMOND, MANCHESTER WALL

On Sunday, November 30, I (Jake Jones) watched as a climber fell approximately 40 feet to the ground while leading. At the time I had just been lowered to the ground after climbing a different route. I happened to look to my right and saw a male climber falling, hit the ground feet-first, and end up in a sitting position.

Luckily, several trained first responders were climbing there that day, along with a nurse. Amazingly, the climber did not seem to have obvious injuries, but he was in tremendous pain. After 911 was called, emergency medical services arrived in under 10 minutes.

ANALYSIS

A number of factors contributed to this incident. The climber appeared to be experienced, but his partner, belaying with an ATC, was new to belaying a leader. The belayer did not brake properly, got her hands burned by the rope, and let go. The leader knew the belayer was inexperienced and chose to hop on lead anyway. Also, she was anchored to the ground with a piece of cord clipped to her harness haul loop. Haul loops are for hauling a second rope on long climbs, not for attaching to anchors. (*Source: Jake Jones.*)

[*Editor's note: Manchester Wall is located by the James River, near downtown Richmond, and consists of three 60-foot granite pillars of an abandoned Richmond and Petersburg Railroad bridge.*]

WASHINGTON

RAPPEL ERROR | No Knots in Rope Ends
MT. GARFIELD, INFINITE BLISS

On September 7, at 5 p.m., Ross Halverson and a partner completed Infinite Bliss, a 23-pitch 5.10c that climbs the south flank of Mt. Garfield, near North Bend. They texted a friend from the summit, took a few photos, then immediately headed back down the route via double-rope rappels. The pair knew they had hours of rappelling before them and only two hours of full daylight remaining.

Near 7 p.m., about halfway down the route (it has been difficult to pinpoint exactly what pitch the two were on), Halverson rigged another rappel and started descending. Presumably to expedite the descent, he knowingly passed the next rappel station and continued toward a lower anchor. The ropes did not reach the next station, however, and Halverson came off the end of the ropes. He fell about three pitches to his death.

ANALYSIS
Fundamentally, this accident could have been avoided by putting knots at the ends of the rappel lines. However, as with many accidents in the mountains, the chain of events and decisions leading up to the accident present a complex case worthy of closer reflection. The stated goal of the two climbers was to do the entire climb in a single day on their first attempt, which is not an unrealistic goal in itself, but as a pair they had never tackled an objective of that scope. It became evident to the climbers about halfway up the route that they were moving slower than desired. It is at this point that they had a "go, no-go" conversation. They decided to continue with full knowledge of the added risk of rappelling at night. At this point the heuristic trap of commitment drove the climbers into a higher risk situation. It can be argued that the desire to rappel as quickly as possible, racing the sun, led to decisions like not placing knots at the end of the rope and skipping a rappel station.

As climbers we make risk calculations, and at times our focus on certain risks— particularly future risks—can blind us to the risks of the present. So too our goals and commitments can trap us into a series of events that have potentially fatal consequences. (*Source: Matthew Denton, climbing guide and friend of the deceased.*)

CREVASSE FALL | Poor Position
NORTH CASCADES NATIONAL PARK, EAST MCMILLAN SPIRE

On July 29, my husband, Arthur Greef (52), and I (Colleen Hinton, 52) left camp at 6:30 a.m. with the goal of climbing the west ridge of East McMillan Spire (Class 3/4), followed by the southeast face of West McMillan Spire (Grade II 5.7). The weather was very warm, continuing a pattern of warmer-than-usual temperatures in the Pacific Northwest this summer. Due to heavy snowmelt, a large and unclimbable gap had formed between the top of the bergschrund and the bottom of the snow finger leading up to the notch between the two spires. After exploring alternatives, we decided to retreat and attempt another route. By this time it was about 9:30 a.m.

While we were trying to locate our alternative route, we saw climbers rappelling down the south face of the east spire and onto the glacier, and we asked them whether the base of the snow finger might be accessible from their rappel route. Receiving an answer in the affirmative, we reascended the glacier and climbed to the lip of the bergschrund to look for the best route to the rock wall. As I was preparing my axe and a picket for a belay, I heard a "whumph" and instinctively grabbed the rope with my bare hands and threw myself onto the snow. I saw that the top of the bergschrund had collapsed under Arthur's weight and he had disappeared below.

Arthur estimates he hit rock within a couple of meters and then slid another eight meters on a wet, low-angled face until his backpack caught him. My hands had a couple of painful burns, but I was able to belay Arthur with a tight rope as he climbed out of the crevasse. He had been injured in the right eye (possibly by his ice axe) and was bleeding from the eye and a laceration on his cheek. We packed snow over the wound and descended to a point where we met the two Canadian climbers who had been rappelling. They examined Arthur and urged us to request a helicopter evacuation.

Although cell service on the mountain was inconsistent, I was able to contact the Marblemount Wilderness Information Center and secure a helicopter for Arthur's rescue. A friend that I reached by text contacted the AAC and Global Rescue. Arthur was flown to Harborview Medical Center by evening, while I hiked out with the Canadians. He went into surgery that night to repair a laceration that extended to the back of the eye. The doctors saved the eye and much of his eyesight.

ANALYSIS

We are each experienced climbers (25-plus years) and should have known better than to get too close to the lip of a melted-out bergschrund in an unusually warm summer. We let our guard down when we saw the two other climbers rappel safely onto the bergschrund in a different spot, and our desire to "stop messing around" and complete a climb that day overtook our earlier caution. We are not convinced that the accident could have been avoided by being on belay, since Arthur hit the rock within a very short distance after he fell. We possibly could have used an ice axe or a trekking pole to test the thickness of the snow at the top of the bergschrund. We are grateful to the Canadian climbers, Chris and Dave, for their support and their insistence on requesting a helicopter rescue, which contributed greatly to a good medical outcome. (*Source: Colleen Hinton.*)

FALL ON ICE | Anchor Failure
SNOQUALMIE PASS, ALPENTAL, KIDDIE CLIFF

On December 3 I left the Alpental parking lot around 10 a.m. with a good friend to find some ice to top-rope. This trip was training for bigger alpine ice objectives to follow in 2015. After about two hours of hiking and hunting, we found a gully with a frozen creek and decided to rope up and ascend it. We simul-climbed through easy 20°–30° ice with occasional steps about eight feet high, placing ice screws along the way.

After a couple of hundred feet we encountered an ice flow that was about 40 feet high with a towering cedar directly above it, and decided it was the perfect location for a top-rope. My partner ascended the gully to the right of the ice and traversed through low-angle terrain covered in shrubs. For an anchor, he tied a 30-foot length of retired climbing rope around the tree with a bowline and attached a locking carabiner to the end of the rope using a figure 8 on a bight. He then rappelled to the base of the ice.

We climbed the ice for the next three hours, each taking at least four laps on different parts of the formation. After my last lap, my partner suggested I climb back up to the anchor to clean it. I agreed and enjoyed a final lap.

At the top, the ice ended at a ledge with three feet of vertical dirt terminating in a 30° slope at about my hip level. The copious shrubbery and thin, powdery snow covering the ground left no purchase for hands or tools to mantel onto the slope. I decided instead to clip my tools to my harness, grasp the end of the rope going down to my partner, and haul myself up the short distance to the anchor. I took a couple steps to my left to get directly in line of pull with the anchor and hauled in about a foot of rope. My belayer took the slack, and I pulled a second time. As I slid my hand up the rope a third time, I felt slack, noticed the bushes above me shaking, and immediately began falling through the air.

I do not remember hitting the ground. I slid down the gully 35 feet until the rope came tight against my belayer, who arrested my fall. I was unconscious for about a minute and came to in a panic, repeatedly asking my belayer, "Did I fall? Where are we?" As I began to grasp the situation, I told him I could not feel my legs.

I was wearing softshell pants, a base layer, thin puffy coat, and hard shell. My partner pulled the bivy pad out of his pack and placed it under me, along with the pack. He carried two puffy coats and placed both around me. Then he said, "I am going for help," and he was gone. It was 4:30 in the afternoon, and the sun was starting to set.

As I lay on the ice I fought to bring my breathing under control. Under my head there was a depression in the ice so I could not rest my head without tilting it back. Considering that I had a badly broken back, this was very uncomfortable. I pulled down the length of rope attached to me and stuffed it behind my head. This improved things somewhat, but I was unable to shift my body and I had to hold my head up with my neck and abdominal muscles. A short while later, I noticed that one of the jackets had blown off me, and I began to feel cold. I knew I had a spinal cord injury and should not move, but I decided that I was more afraid of the cold, and I pushed myself upright until I could grab the jacket and wrap myself in it again.

I watched the colors of the sky change and the stars come out. I began to shake with the cold. Every few minutes, I would call for help. About three hours after my fall, I heard a helicopter in the distance and hoped that it was here for me. I continued to yell for help. Another hour passed, and I began to hear voices far away. A group from the Seattle Mountain Rescue Team soon arrived, climbed up above me, and began to rig some ropes. Soon one of them rappelled down and put me in a cervical collar. I was able to rest my head for the first time in four hours.

The helicopter returned and lowered a paramedic. The team moved me onto a back board, and I was hauled away from the scene and flown straight to the hospital. My injuries included a mild concussion, six broken ribs, and five broken vertebrae, including the displacement of my lower spine, resulting in a severed spinal cord.

ANALYSIS

After hours of discussion with my climbing partner, I believe there are two possibilities to explain the anchor failure. The first was that the screw gate on the single locking carabiner attaching the climbing ropes to the anchor somehow opened as we moved the ropes back and forth, and then my rope popped out of the carabiner as I tried to pull onto the slope below the anchor. The other possibility is that the section of climbing rope used for the anchor either broke or the knot (a bowline) tying this rope around the tree came undone. The anchor was not examined during the night of the accident, and when friends returned several days later the anchor rope was gone, either picked up as trash by the SAR team or by other climbers.

Whichever theory explains the failure of this anchor, there are two primary takeaways: 1) top-rope anchors should have redundancy throughout the system; and 2) anchors should be checked regularly when they are weighted and unweighted during a day of climbing.

I suffered a potentially fatal fall due to an unusual anchor failure. I will likely never walk again, but otherwise I am in good health. I'm lucky that my back broke near the bottom of my spine and not in my neck, so I can still move my fingers and do my job. I'm lucky that I did not suffer a traumatic brain injury, and that I can still recognize my mother and tell her how much I love her. My helmet is missing a chunk of hard plastic, and the inner shock-absorbing material was broken at every intersection. It saved my life. (*Source: Josh Hancock.*)

RAPPEL FAILURE | No Knot on Rope End, Fatigue
NORTH CASCADES, LE PETIT CHEVAL, SPONTANEITY ARÊTE

On September 6 my husband, Eric Peter Anderson (28), and I (27) summited Le Petit Cheval via the Spontaneity Arête (5.7) for our first anniversary. It was a gloriously clear day and we took our time on the route, admiring the views and relishing the wilderness. We descended the climbing route via a combination of several rappels and a rotten gulley, and arrived at the base in early evening. After packing our gear, we began the class 2 or 3 scramble down the lower slopes, looking forward to dinner.

We descended easily to the upper fixed line on the approach route. (There are two hand lines installed along steep areas of the approach.) This hand line had a few core shots—in fact, we had not used it for this reason while climbing up in the morning. Eric arrived a minute or so before me at the line, and he noticed there was a rap station there and began to set up a rappel with our rope. It was 7:15 p.m. Eric rappelled first, tightening his auto-block before he began to descend. Suddenly the rope went whipping through the rappel rings and Eric was falling, bouncing off the rocks like a toy. I screamed his name several times as he fell out of sight. Upon receiving no response, I began calling for help and descended the sketchy hand line.

Several climbers below me had found Eric curled in a heap under the trees that had stopped his fall. When I finally arrived, climbers had already begun descending for help. Two drove to Mazama to call 911. Others stayed on the road and along the trail to guide rescuers. James, Paul, and I stayed with Eric, who was bleeding heavily from the head. There were no vital signs, though James said he felt a faint pulse when he first arrived. We gently elevated Eric's head with my pack, covered him with jackets and a sleeping bag, and waited for rescue. We stayed on the mountain until 11 p.m., when we received word from the sheriff that mountain rescue planned to do a body recovery in the morning by helicopter. I descended to the road with James and Paul.

ANALYSIS

James and Paul examined the rope as we waited for rescuers. It looked as though Eric had only tied a knot in one end. He must not have realized he'd reached the ends of the rope—or the ropes were uneven—and when he hit the single knot the other side of the rope was pulled through the device and the anchor, causing him to fall to the ground. It appeared that he had been killed nearly instantly from severe head and neck trauma. I will never know why Eric did not tie a knot on the second end of the rappel rope. He was an aerospace engineer with ridiculous intelligence, and he was meticulous to the point where it was annoying. However, even the most scrupulous people can forget things when they're tired. It had been a very long day, and I think we had only gotten about five hours of sleep the previous night. Due to fatigue, I think Eric simply forgot to tie the second knot.

The rescue response and kindness from climbers on the mountain that night was indescribable. Thank you to all those who volunteered to help and to the helicopter crew that retrieved Eric's body the following morning. (*Source: Dandelion Dilluvio.*)

FALL ON ICE | Possible Avalanche
MT. RAINIER, LIBERTY RIDGE

On Monday, May 26, an Alpine Ascents International guided party started an ascent of Mt. Rainier via Liberty Ridge. Led by guides Matt Hegeman and Eitan Green, John Mullaly (Seattle), Uday Marty (Singapore), Mark Mahaney (St. Paul), and Erik Kolb (New York) rounded out the team. They planned to bivouac on May 26 at Curtis Ridge and on May 27 at Thumb Rock on Liberty Ridge. They hoped to climb over the summit on May 28 and descend to Camp Schurman.

The AAI team was spotted as they ascended the route on Wednesday, May 28, by an independent party behind them. That evening, at 6:20 p.m., Hegeman called the company's office to report they were going to camp and that the weather was deteriorating. Additionally, two texts, a SPOT tracking device message, and a picture of the Wednesday night camp were sent to friends of the climbers that night. As confirmed by one of the group's SPOT beacons, they were camping at approximately 12,800 feet, near the top of the Black Pyramid, a large rocky feature that is bypassed by climbing a snow and ice slope on the left. Hegeman reported that all was well with the group and they hoped to summit the next day. These were the last messages received from the team.

At approximately 6:30 p.m. on May 30, Enumclaw police dispatch received a call from Alpine Ascents International reporting an overdue team on Liberty Ridge. At Camp Schurman, ranger Stefan Lofgren located and interviewed the pair of climbers who had just completed the Liberty Ridge and had seen the AAI party two days earlier. They told Lofgren that the larger team left Thumb Rock at about 8 a.m. on May 28, and that they had heard a belay signal yelled from above that afternoon. Around 4 p.m. bad weather moved in, and several inches of snow fell over the following hours. As they climbed the route the next day, the pair discovered a smashed ice axe near the base of the Black Pyramid, as well as a second ice axe planted in the snow and a black plastic bag higher up. They saw tracks but could not determine their age or origin.

An NPS-led search was launched early on May 31, with a climbing ranger team ascending the route and a helicopter team doing aerial reconnaissance. Aerial searchers located a broad debris field of climbing and camping gear (estimated at 0.5 mile by 0.25 miles in area) near the base of Willis Wall, 3,000 feet below the last known location of the climbers. No sign of survivors was observed, either by the ground team

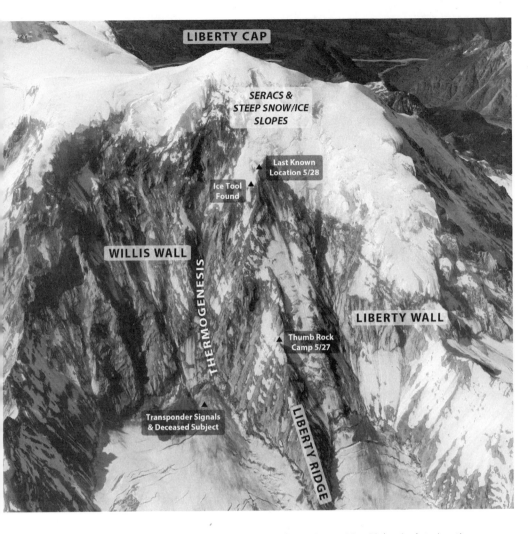

LIBERTY CAP

SERACS &
STEEP SNOW/ICE
SLOPES

Last Known
Location 5/28

Ice Tool
Found

WILLIS WALL

THERMOGENESIS

LIBERTY WALL

Thumb Rock
Camp 5/27

Transponder Signals
& Deceased Subject

LIBERTY RIDGE

[Above] A team of six climbers had hoped to summit Liberty Cap on May 28, but in deteriorating weather they decided to camp near the top of a formation called the Black Pyramid. Sometime that night or early next morning, the entire team appears to have been swept down the Thermogenesis couloir to the upper Carbon Glacier. *Google Earth / NPS Case Incident Record*

that climbed the Liberty Ridge or by aerial searchers. During a second helicopter flight in early afternoon, searchers equipped with avalanche beacons reported multiple beacon signals from the debris field. Again, however, no sign of survivors was observed, and ongoing icefall and rockfall in the area presented an immediate threat to the hovering helicopter or potential ground searchers.

Given the evidence, the NPS concluded that the party had been swept off the mountain, sometime while they were still at their high camp during the night of May 28 or the morning of May 29. Because of the significant risk to recovery teams, the decision was made on the afternoon of May 31 not to attempt immediate recovery of the victims. (*Source: NPS Case Incident Record.*)

ANALYSIS

Liberty Ridge is prone to the standard objective hazards of any big mountain climb, including glacier travel, altitude, weather, rock/ice fall, and avalanches. It remains unclear exactly what caused this accident, but it's likely that an avalanche, icefall, or a collapsing ice ledge swept the climbers off the ridge and down to the Carbon Glacier below the Willis Wall. By all accounts, Matt Hegeman and Eitan Green were climbing guides of the highest caliber. This tragic event reminds us that regardless of how competent trip leaders, partners, or clients may be, the risks inherent in climbing mountains will always be present. (*Source: The Editors.*)

CREVASSE FALL | Climbing Unroped, Inadequate Equipment
MT. RAINIER, MUIR SNOWFIELD

At around 2 p.m. on September 5, a report came in from an RMI guide that he had encountered an independent climber (age approximately 35) who had fallen into a crevasse on the Muir Snowfield at around 9,900 feet. The climber was several feet below the surface and was stemming the two walls of the crevasse, with about 30 feet below his boots to the bottom of the crevasse.

RMI guides helped to extract the suspended climber by reaching into the crevasse and lifting him up and out. Once the climber was on the surface, the guides assessed the patient and noticed a possible shoulder dislocation. With the help of the climber's partner, the guides reduced the possible shoulder dislocation. Rangers then assisted the climber in descending to Paradise, where he was advised to seek medical care. (*Source: Mt. Rainier National Park.*)

ANALYSIS

This incident is presented as a reminder that crevasse falls occur fairly frequently on the Muir Snowfield, where easy access lures many climbers, hikers, and skiers who are unprepared for safe glacier travel. (*Source: The Editors.*)

WEST VIRGINIA

ANIMAL BITE
BOZOO, ICEBERG AREA

On August 30, Jay Sullivan (56) was bitten by a bat (species unknown) while climbing a short trad route called Playing Hookie (5.7). According to the climber, he was unsure whether he had been bitten or if he had jammed his finger awkwardly into the rock, though he heard "clicking" sounds coming from the crack and noticed a small puncture wound on one finger. He descended and then reclimbed the route with a headlamp, whereupon he identified a bat in the crevice. Returning home later that day, he sought medical advice and received post-exposure prophylaxis for rabies.

ANALYSIS

Rabies is a fatal viral disease that must be treated rapidly if suspected. Bats are a major reservoir of rabies in the United States and abroad. If you suspect a bite or scratch by a bat or mammal that could carry rabies take the following steps: 1) clean the wound thoroughly with copious amounts of water and/or povidone-iodine; 2) seek medical evaluation as soon as possible; 3) begin post-exposure prophylaxis if indicated. (*Source: R. Bryan Simon.*)

FALL ON ROCK | Inadequate Protection, No Helmet
NEW RIVER GORGE NATIONAL RIVER, JUNKYARD AREA

On November 9 a male climber (28) was leading New River Gunks, a popular 5.7 traditional route, when he fell approximately 12 to 15 feet. The climber, whose only protection was a single fixed cam (Wild Country Zero 5), suffered a groundfall and landed in a seated position, also hitting his head. The fixed gear, which local guides and climbers noted had been present since at least 2009, failed when the cable stem of the device separated from the cam head assembly during the fall.

Other climbers placed a call to the Fayette County 911 center, and NPS rangers, nearby climbers, and first responders carried the injured climber by litter to the parking area for transport to a local hospital. The climber suffered a spinal injury and fractured his ulna and radius. He was not wearing a helmet. (*Source: Jeff West, Chief Ranger, NPS Morning Report; Frank Sellers, Ranger, NPS Incident Report.*)

ANALYSIS
Although this cam was solidly placed within the crack, the integrity of fixed gear can never be assessed comprehensively. This accident easily could have been avoided by placing additional gear nearby, as there were multiple placements available. (*Source: R. Bryan Simon.*)

WYOMING

SLIP ON SNOW | Inadequate Equipment, Exceeding Abilities
DISAPPOINTMENT PEAK, LAKE LEDGES

Late in the day on June 29, a female climber (27) fell and sustained serious injuries while descending the Lake Ledges route on Disappointment Peak. [*Editor's note: Lake Ledges is a 4th class route in midsummer and a moderate snow climb through spring and early summer.*] Her partner reported that after slipping on a snow slope she tumbled across several rocks and fell to the snow at the base of the climb. The climber was stable but with a possible broken leg.

The initial plan was to locate the victim and, if conditions allowed, conduct a short-haul extraction. A backup plan was to lower the injured climber to a backcountry cache near Surprise Lake and spend the night with her, then fly her out the following morning. Two rangers boarded a helicopter and flew to the accident scene to conduct a size-up. At 8:10 p.m. the rangers reported that, due to high winds, they were unable to conduct a short-haul and were looking for a landing spot on the ridge above the climb. The winds also precluded a landing below the victim near Amphitheater Lake.

Six rangers were flown to the ridge. They climbed down to the victim, evaluated her condition, and determined that she would need to be extricated that evening.

As the six rangers on scene began to lower the victim toward the Surprise Lake switchbacks, four other rangers gathered a wheeled litter and additional equipment. The victim was packaged and lowered by wheeled litter, through intermittent snow and steep trail, all the way to the Lupine Meadows trailhead. From there she was transferred to a waiting ambulance and taken to St. John's Hospital in Jackson.

This complex and physically demanding rescue involved 10 rangers and took almost 10 hours to conduct in darkness over rugged trail. Although the rescue took a toll on equipment, no injuries were reported.

ANALYSIS

The injured climber reported that she and her partner were descending snow when she lost her footing and fell. The victim, equipped with an ice axe and wearing a helmet, was unable to self-arrest as she slid on snow, bounced across a rock area, and dropped over a small cliff to the snow below. Her partner was below her and kicking steps to aid her descent when she fell. Neither climber was wearing crampons.

The climber admitted that her knowledge and experience of mountainous snow travel was very limited and she was climbing outside her abilities. Crampons and, more importantly, knowledge and experience of steep snow travel may have prevented this accident. (*Source: Chris Harder, Incident Commander.*)

ROCKFALL | Failure to Test Holds
GRAND TETON, UPPER EXUM RIDGE ·

On July 27, Joshua Smith and I (both 32) attempted the Grand Teton via the Upper Exum Ridge. While climbing the route, I sustained severe injuries to my left foot when I pulled a loose boulder down. The incident occurred in a section of the climb known as the Wind Tunnel. While surmounting a short wall and pulling onto a ledge, I placed my hand on a large, flat boulder; as I pulled down, the boulder shifted and slid toward me. I quickly fell backward several feet onto a patch of snow, landing on my back with my legs in front of me, my feet pointing outward. The boulder continued to slide and impacted my left foot, mostly near the heel. Based on the size of the boulder I estimate it to have been 800 to 1,000 pounds.

I spent about 30 minutes in shock and extreme pain. I had left my prescription-strength pain medication at camp, but Josh had naproxen, and I took a couple of tablets. After debating what to do, Josh and I chose to "retreat upward," toward the summit, rather than down the route. I managed to support myself enough to stand on my right leg and ease weight onto my left foot. I found I could support about a quarter of my weight on the ball and toes of my foot. We slowly scrambled upward. Below the Friction Pitch, with the help of a doctor in another party, we wrapped my foot in an ACE bandage and tape to stabilize it. My sock was soaked in blood (from two puncture wounds, we later discovered). We continued up the Upper Exum without further incident, with Josh leading all the pitches.

At approximately 2 p.m. we began our descent from the summit via the Owen-Spalding Route, aided down the rappels by another party. By this time my foot and ankle had become extremely swollen and the bandage was soaked with blood. Slowly scrambling down the descent gully, we reached the Lower Saddle at 5:30 p.m., roughly nine hours after the rockfall.

. At the Lower Saddle, we informed Exum Mountain Guides about my situation and discussed with them whether to call for a rescue. Suspecting fractures, I eventually placed a call for rescue and a helicopter arrived 30 minutes later. This carried me down to the valley, and Josh hiked out with all of our gear. The injuries to my left foot included soft-tissue damage, two puncture wounds, and significant bone bruising to my heel, ankle, and toes. There were no fractures.

ANALYSIS

The cause of the accident was my failure to inspect and test holds. I became complacent during the climb, especially during the unroped portions. Although I am an experienced rock climber, I am fairly new to alpine climbing. The hazards in the alpine environment are more numerous and the consequences are more severe, even on a relatively well-traveled climb like the Upper Exum. (*Source: Brett Verhoef.*)

[Above] The Exum Ridge, one of America's most popular alpine rock routes, was the site of three serious accidents in 2014. The scenes of these incidents are labeled. *Erik Lambert*

FALL ON ROCK | Suspected Rockfall, Climbing Alone
GRAND TETON, UPPER EXUM RIDGE

On the morning of August 8, a solo climber sustained life-threatening injuries in a fall while attempting the Grand Teton. Steve Markusen (60) was climbing midway between the Friction Pitch and V-Pitch on the Upper Exum Ridge when the accident occurred. Two climbers in a separate party came upon Markusen, but did not have a cell phone to call for help. They continued to the summit of the Grand Teton, about 400 feet above, where they located other climbers with a cell phone and called the Jenny Lake Ranger Station. In the meantime, another party of two climbers encountered Markusen and began to provide first aid; they too placed a 911 call. They later reported the climber was passing in and out of consciousness and had various lacerations and possible fractures.

About an hour later, while the park's rescue operation was under way, a third climbing party with four firefighters came upon Markusen and the two climbers who were assisting him; two of these climbers had medical training and they stayed with

Markusen to provide advanced medical assistance until park rangers arrived. Due to the threat of an approaching storm, all the other climbers continued to the summit so they could descend.

A helicopter flew seven rangers and a Teton Interagency Helitack Crew member to the Lower Saddle. Because of cloud cover high on the mountain, a ground-based rescue mission commenced. From the Lower Saddle, two rangers made a quick ascent with minimal gear to reach the critically injured climber and continue emergency medical care. Four additional rangers carried all the equipment necessary for a possible extended ground rescue. Fortunately, a break in the weather at around 2 p.m. made it possible for the helicopter to short-haul a ranger and a rescue litter to the accident site, and at about 3 p.m. a ranger and the victim were short-hauled from the site to the Lupine Meadows Rescue Cache.

Markusen's injuries were serious enough to warrant a Life Flight helicopter, but poor weather prevented this flight. Instead, Grand Teton rangers, emergency medical technicians, and paramedics set up a temporary emergency room inside the Jenny Lake Rescue Cache to stabilize Markusen before transporting him by park ambulance to St. John's Medical Center in Jackson. Markusen arrived at the local hospital at 4:20 p.m., over five hours after his fall. (*Source: Jackie Skaggs, Public Affairs Officer.*)

ANALYSIS

Although unable to recall exactly what happened, the climber believes he may have been struck by a rock from above, which caused him to fall or tumble approximately 100 feet down the steep granite slabs above the Friction Pitch. He was not wearing a helmet and incurred extensive traumatic injuries during his tumbling fall. He is lucky other climbers discovered him quickly.

Climbing solo and unroped in the mountains can be a dangerous game. Rockfall, loose ledges, and breakable handholds are characteristics of the Tetons. The Upper Exum is one of the most popular alpine rock climbs in the entire United States—with loose rock present, this creates a dangerous scenario for climbers below.

If this climber had been with a partner and roped up, with protection in place, his fall may have been minimal. If you choose to climb alone and unroped, wear a helmet and make an effort to be among the first on the route, in order to minimize your exposure to rocks knocked off by other climbers. (*Sources: Jackie Skaggs, Public Affairs Officer, George Montopoli, Incident Commander, and the Editors.*)

FALL ON ROCK | Inexperience, Weather, Protection Pulled Out
GRAND TETON, LOWER EXUM RIDGE

On October 5, at approximately 11:15 a.m., a male climber (26) called Grand Teton dispatch to report that his partner (male, 39) had fallen and broken his leg while leading the first pitch of the Lower Exum Ridge. He stated they needed to be rescued. With high winds on the mountain, the party was informed that a helicopter rescue might not be possible and that they should attempt to self-rescue as far as possible.

Because of the severity of the terrain and current conditions on the route, including snow- and ice-covered rock, the rescue was anticipated to be complex. Five rangers and a helicopter were summoned to Lupine Meadows. After a recon of the lower mountain from the air, two rangers were dropped at the Lower Saddle and the helicopter returned to Lupine Meadows to be configured for short-haul operation.

The two rangers at the Lower Saddle made a short climb to the injured climber, who was located just below the chimney on the first pitch of the route. They arrived on scene at 1:48 p.m. At 2:30 p.m., after packaging the injured climber, the rangers requested a short-haul evacuation. The climber and a ranger were extracted at 2:42 p.m. and flown to Lupine Meadows, where the victim was transferred to an ambulance and taken to St. John's Medical Center in Jackson. The other ranger and the climber's partner rappelled from the scene and hiked down to the Lower Saddle, where they met the helicopter and were flown to Lupine Meadows.

ANALYSIS

The Lower Exum Ridge is rated 5.7. The route begins with some low-angle, blocky terrain just above the Black Dike before it transitions into a large, 120-foot 5.7 chimney. This first-pitch chimney is considered the crux of the route. Though this route is not considered difficult for a 5.8–5.9 climber, it can be outright desperate if not climbed in ideal conditions.

The two climbers left their camp at the Caves at about 3:30 a.m. with a plan to climb the complete Exum Ridge. Once they arrived at the Lower Saddle, they came to the conclusion that the entire route would not be feasible. Consequently, they made a plan to only climb the Lower Exum Ridge and exit down Wall Street.

The two made their way toward the base of the Lower Exum and began climbing the snow-covered ramp to the bottom of the first pitch at about 9:30 a.m. [*Editor's note: A six-hour approach from the Caves Camp to the base of this route is quite slow, indicating poor conditions and perhaps a lack of fitness.*] The first climber was leading in boots and crampons at this point. He had placed five or six pieces of protection in a diagonal crack and was working his way upward in the bottom of the chimney when he fell about six feet and was caught by his last cam placement. Unfazed by his fall, he got back on the climb and proceeded upward. He fell again, and this time the cam that caught his previous fall pulled out, causing him to fall much further—about 20 feet.

The climber couldn't recall exactly what caused him to fall for a second time. However, sometime during his fall he either caught his crampon on a rock or his crampon impacted the wall, causing his leg to snap. The victim called down to his partner and told him that he had broken his leg and could not climb down. The partner immediately made a 911 cell phone call for help and initiated a SPOT beacon alert before he began to assist the victim down to the belay ledge.

Both men had been climbing three to four years and considered themselves to be competent on 5.8–5.9 traditional routes, with some mixed climbing experience. They were properly equipped to deal with a variety of conditions (snow, ice, and rock). Unfortunately, on this particular day, the rock on the route was covered with a light dusting of unconsolidated snow and no ice—not conditions for which they were suited. Rangers had conveyed the conditions on the route to the climbers the day before they left. They were also informed that, should they need a rescue, it could be greatly delayed due to lack of staffing and potentially unfavorable weather. It was by sheer coincidence that two seasonal climbing rangers, who had recently concluded their seasons, happened to be in the area of Lupine Meadows when the initial call came in and thus were available to help with the rescue. (*Source: Chris Harder, Incident Commander.*)

CANADA

Unless otherwise noted, reports in this section were drawn from park reports and summaries, and Robert Chisnall of the Alpine Club of Canada provided the analyses. Several additional reports from 2014 may be found at publications.americanalpineclub.org.

ILLNESS

YUKON, KLUANE NATIONAL PARK AND RESERVE, MT. LOGAN, EAST RIDGE

On June 6, at 11 a.m., the Parks Canada Visitor Safety team in Haines Junction received a call regarding a male climber in medical distress and requesting evacuation. The initial call came in via the Delorme InReach coordination center. Fortunately, the party of four climbers also had a satellite phone, and reliable information on the patient's condition, exact location, and weather conditions was quickly conveyed.

The patient was experiencing severe whole-body cramping, dizziness, an altered level of consciousness, and an inability to climb up or down. Their location was at approximately 3,400 meters (11,155 feet) on the east ridge of Logan. This area is just up from a knife-edge ridge at the base of a large snow slope. Weather at the site was clear and calm, and the forecast showed a 10-hour window of clear, stable air before the next unstable weather moved in. A Parks Canada pilot and rescuer flew one hour to the site to assess the terrain and prepare for a rescue. At 3 p.m., the pilot and rescuer were able to toe-in under power, load the patient, and return to Haines Junction. The patient was treated at the local health center for dehydration, electrolyte imbalance, and exhaustion. It remains undetermined if altitude was a complicating factor.

[Below] Approaching a stranded party at 3,400 meters on Mt. Logan's east ridge. *Scott Stewart*

ANALYSIS

The importance of reliable two-way communication in such a remote environment cannot be overstated. A satellite phone allows critical information to flow directly from party leader to rescue leader. This minimizes delays in response or aborted rescue attempts due to poor weather. That said, in remote northern environments, particularly at altitude, parties must be prepared to self-rescue, descend to an accessible location, or wait for considerable delays in organization of a response. Technical rescue resources in this immediate area are limited. In this case, the weather window was perfect. However, it is common to wait days or a week for a storm to clear enough to access the mountain by air. (*Source: Scott Stewart, Visitor Safety/Fire Coordinator.*)

RAPPEL ERROR | Off-Route, Inadequate Equipment
BRITISH COLUMBIA, PENTICTON, SKAHA BLUFFS

On August 30, a 31-year-old man was rappelling his third climb of the day (Fortuitous, 5.10d, on the Fortress) when he fell about 20 meters to the ground and sustained massive trauma. Three local climbers, two of whom were nurses, immediately attended to the fallen climber. One of the responding climbers observed, "He had one strand of rope through his ATC rappel device and the other end was going up to the anchors." The attending climbers observed that the prone climber was breathing but unresponsive. They attempted CPR until EMT personnel arrived on the scene. He did not survive.

ANALYSIS

Those closest to the event expressed two theories to explain the fall. First, the climber may have failed to clip both strands of rope before rappelling. Second, both ends of the rope may not have extended to the ground, and he rappelled off the short end. This is the more likely of the two theories. If he had failed to clip both sides of the rope before weighting the rappel line, the line probably would have pulled through the rappel anchors completely, considering the lengths of the rappel and the rope.

A friend reported in an online forum that the deceased had used a 60-meter rope with no middle marker. The friend also observed that he did not knot the ends of the rope, and that the rappeller was not aware of the correct descent route and thus likely rappelled farther than anticipated.

Fortuitous is a 50-meter rock climb. A single rope will necessitate two rappels to reach the ground. The correct intermediate anchor is located on a route named Perpendiculous, just to the left of Fortuitous. The rappeller headed toward a different anchor, to the right of Fortuitous, that is about 10 meters lower than the correct one. This meant he was attempting a 30-meter rappel with a 60-meter rope, leaving no margin for error. A safer option would be to haul a second rope to the upper anchor to rappel this route. It is also possible to hike down from the top.

FALL ON SNOW | Poor Position
BRITISH COLUMBIA, ROGERS PASS, MT. SIFTON

On July 28, two experienced climbers planned to ascend the southeast ridge (4th class) of Mt. Sifton from their Hermit Meadows camp. The weather conditions were perfect and the climb proceeded as planned. The pair topped out on Sifton's east ridge about 70 vertical meters below and 250 meters horizontally from the summit. Unfortunately, the otherwise easy-looking ridge was blocked by a steep snow dome. With only a single mountaineering axe each, they decided not to attempt the snow dome and abandoned the summit bid.

From this point they decided to scramble down the northeast ridge to the Sifton-Rogers col to reach easier terrain. However, they first were faced with descending about 350 meters of moderately steep snow near the crest of Sifton's glaciated north face. At times the snow was capable of supporting weight, but more often it was poorly bonded and friable. They pitched out the downclimb, using ice screw anchors. After five and a half pitches of insecure snow, the duo made it to rock scrambling terrain and elected to unrope and repack their crampons. As they continued, the ridge presented a number of obstacles. At one point, faced with several options, the team chose the less technical east flank, following the footprints of a previous solo climber. Crampons and ice axes were readied once again, and the first member of the team led down a short snow slope of about 30°–35°. No anchoring options were immediately available, so the downclimb was unroped.

The lead climber was facing outward with his single ice axe in his right hand. His boot penetrated the snow up to about mid-calf. He took three or four steps and then the snow gave way. The climber instinctively rolled over and began aggressive self-arrest action. However, the unconsolidated snow offered little purchase and his speed did not abate. The snow ended and he fell over a three- or four-meter cliff. He tumbled several times and then impacted the slope heavily on his chest. He came to an abrupt stop about 15 meters from a sharp drop-off, about 100 vertical meters above the glacier.

The battered climber was conscious and used his axe to dig out a stable stance. He removed his crampons and called up to his partner, who was about 100 meters above. His partner descended carefully to his position and they assessed their self-rescue options. They decided to move laterally to skier's left about 30 meters to a relatively stable spot where they could build an emergency anchor. Spontaneous rockfall was occurring about every 10 minutes on the face. At this point, the fallen climber felt his body begin to "seize up" and experienced intense pain in his lower legs, limited use of his left arm, impaired balance, and overall pain. They decided to call for rescue.

They made contact with Jasper Dispatch via satellite phone. A Parks Canada crew was mobilized out of Revelstoke, and a team from Glacier National Park Visitor Safety was slung to the site with a helicopter. They were on the scene at 5:40 p.m. With limited remaining daylight, they quickly packaged the patient and slung him from the scene to the rescue base, followed by his partner. The patient was transferred to an ambulance at 8:30 p.m. The final diagnosis, after many X-rays, determined there were no broken bones, probably a torn rotator cuff, and multiple soft tissue injuries. He was extremely bruised.

ANALYSIS

The injured climber was in his early 70s and his partner was in his 50s. Both were fit and had ample experience on moderate mountaineering routes. Considerable planning preceded the climb, and careful decisions were made at each stage of the ascent and descent. The injured climber offered the following analysis of his accident:

(1) The slope in question had an easterly aspect, and it was in shade half the day. The slip may have been due to a weak layer collapsing and poor cohesion within the underlying snow, perhaps over basal facets. The team observed a weakness in a thin snowpack with a northerly aspect, but had found good snowpack cohesion and support on snow slopes with a southern exposure.

(2) Downclimbing while facing in would have been more secure. At the time, neither the steepness of the slope nor the state of the snowpack seemed to require it.

(3) A belay from a solid anchor would have prevented a serious fall. However, at the time, the fallen climber determined there was no suitable anchor in the area.

According to Danyelle Magnan of Glacier National Park, the group chose to follow another party's tracks but did not consider that the snow conditions might have changed. Due to the late time of day, the snow was wet and loose. Crossing the snow slope exposed them to large cliffs below.

It should be noted that the pair endeavored to assess their situation objectively and considered self-rescue. When this was clearly not feasible, they made the correct decision in calling for help and were able to do so immediately with their sat phone.

ROCKFALL

BRITISH COLUMBIA, YOHO NATIONAL PARK, WIWAXY PEAK

On August 14 two climbers set out from Lake O'Hara to climb the Grassi Ridge on Wiwaxy Peak. Late in the afternoon, light rain began falling, which made the quartzite very slippery and slowed their progress. As they were approaching the final pitch, the leader passed a small pillar that collapsed, sending several large blocks down the climb. The belayer was struck on the thigh with considerable force, causing injuries that prevented him from moving. Their ropes were badly damaged. The leader was able to rappel down on the better of the two ropes and attend to the belayer. The leader called for help using a SPOT satellite communicator and also radioed down to friends at the Lake O'Hara Lodge.

At 8:40 p.m., Visitor Safety staff was notified about the incident. Due to the poor weather and limited daylight, the Visitor Safety team was unable to reach the injured climber that evening. After looking at the weather forecast and communicating with the climbers through the Lake O'Hara lodge, they decided a rescue attempt would be

[Top] The Grassi Ridge is the sun-shadow line in right center. The climbers were rescued from a large ledge near the top. *Dougald MacDonald*

made at first light. The climbers were able to find some shelter under a boulder and wait. Early the next morning the two climbers were slung out by helicopter to a waiting ambulance, where they were treated for mild hypothermia and the injury to the thigh.

ANALYSIS

Falling rock is always a concern on longer rock and alpine routes. Whenever possible, try to place protection to keep the rope from running over loose rock, and seek out sheltered belays to minimize the chances of injury from rockfall.

This case highlights the fact that a rescue can be significantly delayed due to the time of day, as well as weather and route conditions. Having some spare clothing (gloves, hat, jacket) and a light emergency tarp can make a significant difference to a stranded team. This party's ability to communicate effectively with people on the ground was a real bonus, allowing them to convey their location and condition, and allowing rescuers to let them know when to expect a rescue and to monitor their condition through the night.

FALL ON ICE | Inadequate Protection, Screw Pulled Out
ALBERTA, BANFF NATIONAL PARK, LOUISE FALLS

On February 27 a party of two was climbing the classic multi-pitch ice route up Louise Falls (WI4/5). They had climbed the crux pillar and were on the easier last pitch. The less experienced climber attempted to lead this pitch but found it was too much for him, so he lowered back to the belay off a single ice screw. The more experienced leader took over, led past the ice screw, put in another screw, and continued toward the top. As he was climbing over the final bulge, his feet blew out and his tools, which were not set well, popped out of the ice. He fell and pulled out the top screw. The next screw down held his fall. He fell approximately 12 to 15 meters and caught his foot on the ice, breaking his lower right leg. It was 4 p.m. The injured climber was in a lot of pain and the team could not move, so the climbers started yelling for help.

Banff Dispatch got the call from some bystanders on the trail underneath the ice climb. Two Visitor Safety (VS) specialists responded by helicopter from Banff, and two responded by snowmobile from Lake Louise. VS specialists attempted to heli-sling into the patient site, but called off this effort due to overhead tree hazards. The second plan was to sling to the top of the climb with rescue equipment and get ready for a ground evacuation that would last into the night. A single VS specialist was slung to the top of the climb and, with the aid of a guide who happened to be on top, was lowered to the patient's location. The remaining three VS specialists arrived on top with the rest of the rescue gear and belayed the uninjured partner as he climbed up and out. A decision was made to raise the patient to the top of the climb and then lower him down the walk-off route to avoid exposing the rescue team to large hanging ice daggers to the right of the climb. A VS specialist lowered to the site with the stretcher and leg splints and packaged the patient to be raised to the top.

VS specialists were in communication with a doctor at the Banff hospital who advised realignment of the injured limb and nitrous oxide for pain management, both of which were applied to the patient once he reached the top of the climb, with positive results. The patient was then pulled through the forest on a stretcher and lowered to the shore of Lake Louise, which was a long and arduous process for everyone involved.

ANALYSIS

Lead falls while ice climbing often result in serious injuries. The leader should be well within the margins of his or her climbing ability. But accidents happen, which is why it is essential to protect frequently to limit the consequences of a fall. Often, the trickiest part of an ice climb is at the top of a pitch, where you transition from steep to lower angled terrain. It is difficult to see your feet and the ice may be brittle or thin at the top. It is essential to move in control and protect yourself well at the top-out.

FALL ON ICE | Inadequate Protection

ALBERTA, GHOST RIVER VALLEY, MALIGNANT MUSHROOM

On the morning of March 15, two very experienced climbers set out to attempt a series of climbs in the Ghost River Valley. After starting up the first pitch of Malignant Mushroom (WI5), the lead climber fell while placing his first ice screw. He fell about six meters to the base of the climb and slid a short distance, injuring his back. The belayer pushed the 911 button on both of the climbers' SPOT devices to call for a rescue. He

then assessed the climber's injuries, insulated him from the ice, covered the patient with an emergency tarp, and used a stove to fill hot water bottles to place around the patient, helping to prevent hypothermia.

At 9 a.m., Banff Visitor Safety (VS) received the coordinates of the location. The SPOT signals were canceled at one point and then reactivated, which caused a minor delay. After phoning the numbers accompanying the SPOT registration, VS staff were able to confirm that the owners of the SPOT devices were ice climbing in the Ghost River Valley.

At about 11 a.m. the patient was located at the base of the ice climb. Four rescuers slung into the site by helicopter and packaged the injured climber. At 1:45 p.m. the patient was slung out to a staging area and transferred to a STARS Air Ambulance for transport to the hospital in Calgary. His injuries included four fractured vertebrae and a large hematoma on his hip.

ANALYSIS

Despite having all the skills needed for a climb, accidents can happen to anyone. This party was well-prepared. They told friends where they were going, brought appropriate equipment, and had emergency communication devices. The belayer did a good job of providing first aid.

One contributing factor in this event may have been the intense sun the ice climb had received over the previous several days, making the ice surface less secure than normal. The climber was forced to climb higher to find quality ice for his first ice screw, and his tool placements were not optimal. A second contributing factor may have been that the ice tools he used that day were not his regular tools. As a result, he may not have had the same "feel" for the placements as he usually did. A third influence may have been the fact that the group had an ambitious day of climbing planned. As a result, there was some pressure to move quickly on the climb.

The final lesson is that once an emergency signaling device is activated, it is best to leave it on until help arrives to avoid any delays.

ROCKFALL | Poor Position
ALBERTA, YAMNUSKA, MISSIONARY'S CRACK

On June 6 a climber was struck in the lower right leg by a large falling block while climbing Missionary's Crack (5.10) . This was roughly in the area where a major rockfall occurred in August 2009. Two Kananaskis Public Safety personnel were heli-slung to a ledge below the climbers, where they built an anchor. Rescue personnel climbed up to the patient, splinted him, and lowered him to the new anchor, from which he was heli-slung down to a staging area and awaiting EMS personnel.

ANALYSIS
Yamnuska's limestone is known for loose rock, and on this particular route a large pillar collapsed in 2009, destroying most of the fourth pitch and strewing rock over the lower pitches. This once-popular climb should be undertaken with extreme caution or avoided altogether, and this incident is a good reminder of the value of researching recent conditions before attempting a serious climb. Guidebook author Andy Genereux publishes updates on Yamnuska at his website: ghostriverproductions.ca.

FALL ON SNOW | Poor Position
ALBERTA, BANFF NATIONAL PARK, MORAINE LAKE, 3/3.5 COULOIR

A party of two decided to climb the 3/3.5 Couloir (so named because it lies between peaks 3 and 3.5 in the Valley of the 10 Peaks), located at the far end of Moraine Lake. It was July 15 and had been a fairly warm and dry summer in the Rockies, so the couloir was only partly covered in ice and snow. They left the parking lot at 11 a.m. with the intention of climbing as high as the snow coverage would allow and then turning around. While descending around 3 p.m., they decided to glissade. They both lost control in the soft, unconsolidated snow and fell several hundred meters down the couloir. A hiker witnessed the fall and reported it to the front desk staff at the Moraine Lake Lodge, who in turn called Banff Dispatch.

A coordinated response from Visitor Safety (VS) staff in Banff and Lake Louise was mobilized. One climber was uninjured, and the other was still mobile but had unknown injuries. Both subjects were able to self-evacuate to the bottom of the technical terrain, and they were picked up by a rescue helicopter and transported to the ambulance at Moraine Lake.

ANALYSIS
The 3/3.5 Couloir is a steep, 900-meter snow and ice slope that is sometimes skied in the spring. It was once popular in the summer as an access to the Mt. Fay area.

However, the 3/3.5 Couloir is subject to a high amount of rockfall, especially when rocks emerge from under snow in dry summers. Because there are two other well-used and safer access routes to the Mt. Fay area (the Perren and Schiesser/Lomas routes), the 3/3.5 couloir is not recommended in summer. Luckily for them, the climbers were not hit by rocks and the soft snow still present in the gully decreased their total fall distance, preventing more serious injuries.

ROCKFALL | Off-Route, No Helmet
ALBERTA, MT. CORY

On August 25, my climbing partner and I had decided to try a seemingly simple mountain named Mt. Cory. [*The south ridge of Cory is rated an easy/moderate scramble in Alan Kane's Scrambles in the Canadian Rockies guidebook.*] After much evaluation we could not figure out the right way to head up. Due to being off-route, the route was more difficult than expected but was still reasonably within our abilities. After navigating through cliff bands, we ended up following the right route on the upper part of the mountain. Getting to the summit was pretty mellow.

On the way down we went the same way we came up. It was late in the day and the route down was a bit dicier due to the slight variation. After navigating more cliff bands, we were getting closer to easier slopes when my partner, above me, knocked off a three-foot-wide boulder. He screamed "Rock!" and I immediately ran across the 3rd class terrain, doing my finest alpine dodge. But the rock happened to bounce the wrong way. I got hit in the head, fell face-first, and started tumbling down the mountain. As I tumbled out of view I broke many bones, including my upper back, a pinkie finger, and collarbone, and got a puncture wound in my side.

Five minutes later, I woke up covered in blood. I had no idea how I got there, what I was doing, or what country I was in. My partner helped me get my shoe back on and back onto my feet. The descent was the scariest time of my life. I became faintish at times and often didn't know where I was. The scramble was a struggle, having broken bones on both arms. At one point I wasn't sure if I could catch myself as I slid down more steep gravel.

Once we were beyond the cliff bands it was a matter of being careful and making it down to the hospital in time. Mosquitoes kept biting me as I carefully scrambled down to safety. An hour later we arrived back at the car. I was excited to make it out alive. We quickly rushed to the hospital, which ended up being a four-day ordeal. (*Source: Joshua Lewis.*)

ANALYSIS
Several factors should be considered in assessing these events. First and foremost, confirming and following the correct route, using accurate and up-to-date route information, might have helped the climbers avoid unstable ground. Avoid being directly above or below another climber on loose terrain. The climber's partner reported that he had waited until his partner was 15 feet below him and off to the right before moving, but the falling rock unfortunately took a bad bounce. The climbers also said they wished they had brought helmets, which might have reduced the severity of the injured climber's head and facial injuries.

STATISTICAL TABLES

TABLE I
REPORTED CLIMBING ACCIDENTS

Year	Number of Accidents Reported		Total Persons Involved		Injured		Fatalities	
	USA	CAN	USA	CAN	USA	CAN	USA	CAN
1951	15	n/a	22	n/a	11	n/a	3	n/a
1952	31	n/a	35	n/a	17	n/a	13	n/a
1953	24	n/a	27	n/a	12	n/a	12	n/a
1954	31	n/a	41	n/a	31	n/a	8	n/a
1955	34	n/a	39	n/a	28	n/a	6	n/a
1956	46	n/a	72	n/a	54	n/a	13	n/a
1957	45	n/a	53	n/a	28	n/a	18	n/a
1958	32	n/a	39	n/a	23	n/a	11	n/a
1959	42	2	56	2	31	0	19	2
1960	47	4	64	12	37	8	19	4
1961	49	9	61	14	45	10	14	4
1962	71	1	90	1	64	0	19	1
1963	68	11	79	12	47	10	19	2
1964	53	11	65	16	44	10	14	3
1965	72	0	90	0	59	0	21	0
1966	67	7	80	9	52	6	16	3
1967	74	10	110	14	63	7	33	5
1968	70	13	87	19	43	12	27	5
1969	94	11	125	17	66	9	29	2
1970	129	11	174	11	88	5	15	5
1971	110	17	138	29	76	11	31	7
1972	141	29	184	42	98	17	49	13
1973	108	6	131	6	85	4	36	2
1974	96	7	177	50	75	1	26	5
1975	78	7	158	22	66	8	19	2
1976	137	16	303	31	210	9	53	6
1977	121	30	277	49	106	21	32	11
1978	118	17	221	19	85	6	42	10
1979	100	36	137	54	83	17	40	19
1980	191	29	295	85	124	26	33	8
1981	97	43	223	119	80	39	39	6

Year	Number of Accidents Reported		Total Persons Involved		Injured		Fatalities	
	USA	CAN	USA	CAN	USA	CAN	USA	CAN
1982	140	48	305	126	120	43	24	14
1983	187	29	442	76	169	26	37	7
1984	182	26	459	63	174	15	26	6
1985	195	27	403	62	190	22	17	3
1986	203	31	406	80	182	25	37	14
1987	192	25	377	79	140	23	32	9
1988	156	18	288	44	155	18	24	4
1989	141	18	272	36	124	11	17	9
1990	136	25	245	50	125	24	24	4
1991	169	20	302	66	147	11	18	6
1992	175	17	351	45	144	11	43	6
1993	132	27	274	50	121	17	21	1
1994	158	25	335	58	131	25	27	5
1995	168	24	353	50	134	18	37	7
1996	139	28	261	59	100	16	31	6
1997	158	35	323	87	148	24	31	13
1998	138	24	281	55	138	18	20	1
1999	123	29	248	69	91	20	17	10
2000	150	23	301	36	121	23	24	7
2001	150	22	276	47	138	14	16	2
2002	139	27	295	29	105	23	34	6
2003	118	29	231	32	105	22	18	6
2004	160	35	311	30	140	16	35	14
2005	111	19	176	41	85	14	34	7
2006	109	n/a	227	n/a	89	n/a	21	n/a
2007	113	n/a	211	n/a	95	n/a	15	n/a
2008	112	n/a	203	n/a	96	n/a	19	n/a
2009	126	n/a	240	n/a	112	n/a	23	n/a
2010	185	n/a	389	n/a	151	n/a	34	n/a
2011	157	n/a	348	n/a	109	n/a	29	n/a
2012	140	15	309	36	121	12	30	2
2013	143	11	283	24	100	5	21	4
2014	112	10	170	19	89	8	28	1
TOTAL:	7,308	994	13,548	2,082	6,120	740	1,593	299

TABLE II
ACCIDENTS BY LOCATION

Geographical Districts	1951–2013			2014		
	Number of Accidents	Deaths	Total Persons Involved	Number of Accidents	Deaths	Total Persons Involved
Canada*						
Alberta	539	145	1063	6	0	10
British Columbia	321	122	658	3	1	5
Yukon Territory	38	28	79	1	0	4
New Brunswick	1	0	0	n/a	n/a	n/a
Ontario	38	9	68	1	0	1
Quebec	31	10	63	n/a	n/a	n/a
East Arctic	8	2	21	n/a	n/a	n/a
West Arctic	2	2	2	n/a	n/a	n/a
Practice Cliffs[1]	20	2	36	n/a	n/a	n/a
United States						
Alaska	589	216	965	8	1	17
Arizona, Nevada, Texas	115	20	204	2	3	5
Atlantic–North	1113	154	1893	6	2	6
Atlantic–South	204	41	349	12	1	16
California	1460	310	797	34	5	53
Central	138	18	226	1	0	1
Colorado	916	239	2563	18	1	24
Montana, Idaho, South Dakota	94	38	150	4	2	5
Oregon	239	123	520	6	2	9
Utah, New Mex.	198	65	355	8	2	12
Washington	2017	328	1066	8	8	15
Wyoming	615	149	1132	5	1	7

*No data from 2006–2011; includes new data from 2012–2014

Accident numbers from the Mohonk Preserve (Shawangunks) in New York were not provided for 2014, so regional totals are lower than historical averages.

[1]This category includes bouldering, artificial climbing walls, buildings, and so forth. The Practice Cliffs category has been removed from the U.S. data.

TABLE III
ACCIDENTS BY CAUSE

	1951–2013 USA	*1959–2013 CAN.	2014 USA	2014 CAN.
Terrain				
Rock	5036	546	84	4
Snow	2582	362	25	3
Ice	290	15	4	2
River	22	3	1	0
Unknown	22	10	0	1
Ascent or Descent				
Ascent	4066	598	66	5
Descent	1275	385	35	5
Unknown	259	13	9	0
Other[1]	21	0	5	0
Immediate Cause				
Fall or slip on rock	3987	297	55	1
Slip on snow or ice	1140	210	12	3
Falling rock, ice, or object	677	141	11	3
Exceeding abilities	583	36	7	0
Illness[2]	444	26	6	1
Stranded	388	60	4	0
Avalanche	323	128	4	0
Rappel Failure/Error[3]	366	52	16	1
Exposure	281	14	1	0
Loss of control/glissade	228	17	3	1
Nut/cam pulled out	284	11	7	0
Failure to follow route	245	35	10	0
Fall into crevasse/moat	185	52	3	0
Faulty use of crampons	124	7	0	0
Piton/ice screw pulled out	95	13	0	0
Ascending too fast	73	0	1	0
Skiing[4]	68	14	2	0
Lightning	67	7	1	0
Equipment failure	16	3	1	0

	1951–2013 USA	*1959–2013 CAN.	2014 USA	2014 CAN.
Other[5]	615	38	6	0
Unknown	64	10	3	0
Contributory Causes				
Climbing unroped	1064	169	16	0
Exceeding abilities	1012	206	14	0
Placed no/inadequate protection	871	98	15	2
Inadequate equipment/clothing	740	72	8	1
Weather	526	73	11	0
Climbing alone	442	72	10	0
No helmet	375	72	6	1
Inadequate belay[6]	268	28	13	0
Nut/cam pulled out	217	32	8	0
Poor position	231	21	9	3
Darkness	171	21	6	0
Party separated	130	12	5	0
Failure to test holds	111	38	6	1
Piton/ice screw pulled out	86	13	0	1
Failed to follow directions	71	13	6	3
Exposure	66	16	1	0
Illness[2]	40	9	0	0
Equipment failure	13	7	6	0
Other[5]	307	100	1	0
Age of Individuals				
Under 15	1248	12	0	0
15-20	1327	204	9	0
21-25	1544	257	17	1
26-30	1456	211	14	0
31-35	2127	115	12	1
36-50	3476	143	19	0
Over 50	384	34	20	1
Unknown	2171	562	31	7
Experience Level				
None/Little	1913	308	5	0
Moderate (1 to 3 years)	1768	357	29	1

	1951–2013 USA	*1959–2013 CAN.	2014 USA	2014 CAN.
Experienced	2343	451	39	4
Unknown	2445	576	47	5
Month of Year				
January	261	25	4	0
February	232	55	3	1
March	366	70	7	1
April	467	40	13	0
May	1008	65	13	0
June	1236	70	11	2
July	2076	264	13	2
August	1157	192	14	4
September	2041	76	12	0
October	508	42	6	0
November	232	20	5	0
December	126	24	3	0
Unknown	20	1	7	0
Type of Injury/Illness (Data since 1984)				
Fracture	1576	233	45	3
Laceration	822	76	10	0
Abrasion	402	78	9	1
Bruise	583	85	13	4
Sprain/strain	476	35	4	1
Concussion	322	30	11	0
Hypothermia	177	18	2	1
Frostbite	148	12	3	0
Dislocation	163	16	4	0
Puncture	54	13	1	1
Acute Mountain Sickness	48	0	2	0
HAPE	86	0	3	0
HACE	32	0	1	0
Other[7]	416	52	11	1
None	365	199	3	2

N.B. Data change: The 1986 and 1997 editions had some repeat data from previous years. The corrections are reflected in the cumulative data.

[1] Some accidents happen when climbers are at the top or bottom of a route, not climbing. They may be setting up a belay or rappel, or are just not anchored when they fall. This category was created in 2001. The category "unknown" is primarily because of solo climbers.

[2] These illnesses/injuries, which led directly or indirectly to an accident, included HAPE, AMS, chest pain, HACE, and dehydration.

[3] These included inadequate anchors, uneven ropes, no knots in rope ends, inadequate anchor tethers, and rappelling past the anchor (ropes too short).

[4] This category covers ski mountaineering. Backcountry ski touring or snowshoeing incidents, including those involving avalanches, are not counted in these tables.

[5] These included failure to self-arrest, falling off a ledge while unanchored, rope came unclipped from slings, misuse of pulley on Tyrolean traverse, cornice collapse, and anchor failure.

[6] These included lowering errors, miscommunication, ineffective belay, and no belay.

[7] These included internal injuries, chest pain, torn ligaments, burns, hearing loss, digital avulsion, spinal cord injuries, collapsed lung, TBI, unspecified head trauma, eye injury, bat bite, dehydration, and torn rotator cuff.

Note: Injuries are counted only once in each category for a given incident. For example, an accident that results in three broken bones will only be listed once under "Fracture."

CHARTS

COMPILED FROM U.S. ACCIDENT DATA 1951–2014

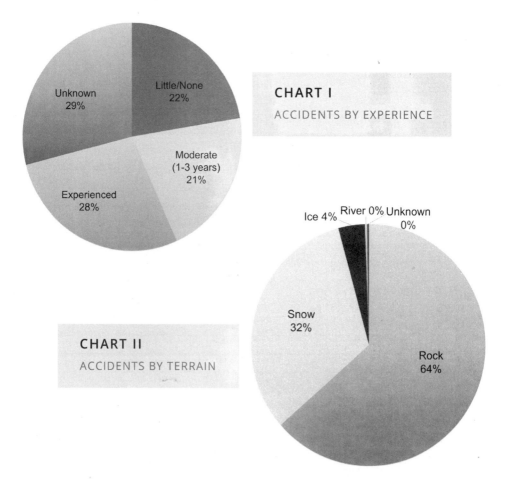

CHART I

ACCIDENTS BY EXPERIENCE

- Unknown 29%
- Little/None 22%
- Moderate (1-3 years) 21%
- Experienced 28%

CHART II

ACCIDENTS BY TERRAIN

- Ice 4%
- River 0%
- Unknown 0%
- Snow 32%
- Rock 64%